Annotated Editio
of the
HISTORY OF THE JONES FAMILY
by
John L. Jones

and

IN MEMORIAM:
J. McHENRY JONES

Edited and Annotated
by

Nancy E. Aiken and
Michel S. Perdreau

Word processed in Times Roman
by
LaVerne Peterson

HERITAGE BOOKS
2012

HERITAGE BOOKS
AN IMPRINT OF HERITAGE BOOKS, INC.

Books, CDs, and more—Worldwide

For our listing of thousands of titles see our website
at
www.HeritageBooks.com

Published 2012 by
HERITAGE BOOKS, INC.
Publishing Division
100 Railroad Ave. #104
Westminster, Maryland 21157

International Standard Book Numbers
Paperbound: 978-0-7884-1877-8
Clothbound: 978-0-7884-3426-6

TABLE OF CONTENTS

Page

INTRODUCTION TO THE ANNOTATED
EDITION OF
The History of the Jones Family   v

GENEALOGICAL CHART OF THE
JONES FAMILY

The Jones Family   vi

Slater Family Chart   xiii

HISTORY of the JONES FAMILY   xiv

Preface   xv

The Story of the Jones Family   1

Notes   53

IN MEMORIAM   67

Biographical Sketch of
J. McHenry Jones   68

Funeral Oration Delivered by
Dr. I. V. Bryant, Pastor of the
First Baptist Church,
Huntington, West Virginia   73

A Eulogy by W. L. Houston, Grand
Master of the Grand United Order
of Odd Fellows   78

President J. McHenry Jones, A.M.,
Litt. D., Scholar and Teacher   80

TABLE OF CONTENTS, cont'd

Page

A Tribute by Hon. H. C. McWhorter,
of the West Virginia Supreme
Court of Appeals   84

An Estimate of J. McHenry Jones
by Governor Wm. E. Glasscock   85

Resolutions Adopted by the Faculty
of the West Virginia Colored
Institute   85

Resolutions of the State Board
of Regents, The Epworth League
and the Enthronement   88

Notes   91

REFERENCES   94

INDEX   98

HISTORY OF THE JONES FAMILY

The 27 January 1894 edition of *The Freeman, An Illustrated Colored Newspaper*, contained a "Plea for Negro Folk Lore." The author exhorted African-Americans to tell their family traditions and histories because future generations would find them valuable. Stories were to be sent to Miss A. M. Bacon of Hampton, Virginia. The stories Miss Bacon received were printed in a Hampton newspaper and, indeed, would be valuable today as, perhaps, the earliest examples of African-American family histories. In 1913 the Rev. Theophilus G. Steward and William Steward published their genealogy of the "people of color" of Gouldtown, New Jersey. Gouldtown provides a genealogy of the forbears of the town's inhabitants focusing more on the unique quality of the town than on its people. It was not until 1930 that a book was published in this country detailing the history of an African-American family from the arrival of the immigrant to the date of publication. John L. Jones probably wrote this narrative about his very successful family because he, like Miss Bacon, felt future generations would find it valuable and also because he was justifiably proud of his family's accomplishments.

Driven to achieve, no doubt, by the general prejudice and low status given African-Americans, the Jones family saw education as its way to freedom and equality. Obviously bright, the family members sought and achieved one advanced degree after another. The Jones family produced doctors and dentists and, especially, educators. The author's brother, James, was the president of what is now West Virginia State College at Institute, West Virginia. An impassioned orator, extracts from his last public speech printed in his memorial (reprinted here) illustrate the strength of his writing and reasoning. John, the author, and his father before him were successful businessmen.

Self-published and with a small run of about 100 copies, *The History of the Jones Family*, nevertheless, had an impact. It was extensively cited by E. Franklin Frazier in his influential *The Free Negro Family: A Study of Family Origins Before the Civil War* (Nashville: Fisk University Press, 1932). It was also cited in a 1977 work, *Black Genealogy*, by Charles L. Blockson.

Mr. Blockson in personal correspondence with Michel S. Perdreau referred to the little book as a "rare historical item" and urged its reprinting because it would be "an asset to genealogical studies for scholars as well as the general public." Mr. Perdreau was able to find only one extant copy of *The History of the Jones Family*. Its owner, a Jones family descendant, has graciously allowed us to publish this new edition.

The History of the Jones Family recounts from oral family tradition the story of six generations of a free black family in America. Most of the information is firsthand knowledge of the author about his immediate family. He was careful to include only dates and data that he felt were correct. However, some discrepancies exist with regard to the information in his brother's memorial. Generally, however, the supporting evidence Mr. Perdreau has found corroborates John L. Jones's narrative.

Jones's narration places his family squarely in the history of their time. Before the Civil War the author's father, Joseph Jones, was a conductor on the Underground Railroad in Gallipolis, Ohio, on the Ohio River across from what was then the slave state of Virginia. Jones's account, undoubtedly from stories told by his parents, is a valuable addition to the literature on the Railroad. His story of the war period itself offers an African-American's perspective of the events. The entire book provides insight into the character of a black family probably not unlike many others who strove for dignity and respect and worked quietly within society's parameters for freedom and equality.

GENEALOGICAL CHART OF THE JONES FAMILY

This chart was devised from the information in John L. Jones's *The History of the Jones Family*, census records and an undocumented family chart (a copy is appended). It uses the National Genealogical Society's revised register system, the directions for which are explained by this example:

Reuben Jones[1] <---indicates generation number; 1 is the progenitor, 2 is the next generation from the progenitor

Issue: +1 i John[2] Jones

The + means that more information on this person will follow. The Arabic numeral is the individual number assigned to this person only. Numbers are generally assigned in sequence with no two people getting the same number. The lower case Roman numeral indicates birth order of the individual. Again, the Arabic numeral following the name of the first born (this number is not repeated for each sibling) indicates the number of generations away from the progenitor. (It does not denote a footnote.) Therefore, John Jones was the eldest child of the progenitor, Reuben Jones.

THE JONES FAMILY

Reuben[1] Jones born ca. 1784-1795 VA; died ca. 1859 OH.
Married Elizabeth Ailstock who was born ca. 1784-1804 and died before 1850; the daughter of Joseph Ailstock.

Issue:	+1	i?	John[2] Jones	born ca. 1815 VA
	+2	ii?	Joseph Jones	born ca. 1825 VA
	+3	iii?	Mary Jones	born 1816-1830? VA
	+4	iv?	Martha Jones	born 1816-1830? VA

1. John[2] Jones born ca. 1815 VA and died after 1880, probably in Jackson Co., OH.
Married Rachel Norman who was born ca. 1824 in VA and died after 1880. [Her surname is assumed from the 1880 census entry (p. 65C Jackson Twp., Jackson Co., OH) which has Sarah Norman as John's mother-in-law, born ca. 1795 in VA.]

Issue:	5	i	Joseph[3] Jones. Born probably 1840s since John L. Jones stated that he served in the Civil War.
	6	ii	Octavia Jones
	7	iii	Oteria Jones. A school teacher.
	8	iv	Emma Jones
	9	v	William Jones. A farmer.
	10	vi	Elizabeth Jones. Married a Mr. Hill and had six children; 3 sons were mechanics in Columbus.
	11	vii	Sylvanis Jones. A farmer.
	12	viii	Edward Jones. Born ca. 1861 in OH (1880 census) [All of the older children were gone from home by the 1880 census.]
	13	ix	Reuben Jones. Born ca. 1863, OH (1880 census); an engineer and teacher.
	14	x	Maria Jones. Born ca. 1865, OH (1880 census); a teacher.
	15	xi	George Jones. Born ca. 1867, OH (1880 census); a teacher.

16   xii   (John) Marshall Jones. Born ca. 1869, OH (1880 census); had 10 children, died ca. 1929-1930.

2. Joseph² Jones. Born ca. 1825, VA (*1860 Federal Census, Gallipolis Twp., Gallia Co., OH*, p. 502); died 13 Dec 1904 Institute, WV.

Married 16 Nov 1847 (*Lawrence Co., OH, Marriages, Bk 4*, p. 90) Temperance Reed, born 15 May 1824, Burlington, OH, to William and Nancy Reed. She died 14 July 1905. Institute, WV. Both are buried in Beechwood Cemetery, Pomeroy, OH.

Issue: 17   i   William Henry⁴ Jones
                    Born ca. 1848, Lawrence Co., OH; died ca. 1857.

  +18   ii   Alexander Jones
                    Born Sept 1851, OH.

   19   iii   Joseph (*1860 Census, Gallipolis Twp., Gallia Co., OH*, p. 502) /Josephus Jones, born 1854; died 1874 of consumption.

  +20   iv   John Lysandrous Jones, born 13 July 1857, Meigs Co., OH (1860 census has "Lander")

          v   *In Memoriam* has James as the 6th child of 10 children and *The History of the Jones Family* has Fleming as the 7th child; there seems to be a child missing. Perhaps a stillborn).

   21   vi   James (Mc)Henry Jones. Born 30 Aug 1859, Gallipolis, OH; died 22 Sept 1909. Married (1) Carrier Harrison of Marietta, OH, in 1888. She died by 1893. Married (2) Elizabeth Moore of Cincinnati in 1893. James had no children. He was president of West Virginia State College at Institute and was renowned as an orator and author. A memorial tribute to him is appended.

  +22   vii   Fleming Bertram Jones. Born 25 Feb 1862, Gallipolis, OH.

  +23   viii   Charles Jones. Born 13 May 1865, Southpoint, OH.

   24   ix   Daughter. Born in New Richmond, OH, but lived only a few days.

   25   x   Thomas Jefferson Jones. Born 7 Aug 1870, Pomeroy, OH; died 15 Oct 1905. Was a dentist in Cleveland, OH. No marriage; buried Beechwood Cemetery, Pomeroy, OH.

3. Mary[2] Jones.   Born 1825 in VA; married Flemmon Bryant.

Issue: 26   i   Charles[3] Bryant. A house mover and contractor. He had a son, Charles, a businessman in Columbus, OH; died before 1930.
27   ii   Abraham Bryant; died before 1930.
28   iii Joseph Bryant. A Columbus policeman who died before 1930.
29   iv   Fleming Bryant; died before 1930.
30   v   James Bryant

4. Martha[2] Jones. Probably Reuben's youngest daughter; possibly born between 1824 and 1830 in VA (*1840 Federal Census, Raccoon Township, Gallia County, OH*, p. 17); married a Mr. Love.

Issue: 31   i   Fannie Lee[3] Love
32   ii   Robert Love
[The census records for Reuben Jones (*1840 Census, Gallia Co.*, as above, and *1850 Census, Lawrence Co., OH, Fayette Twp.*, p. 88) and for Robert Love (*1860 Census, Lawrence Co., OH, Fayette Twp.*, p. 28) complicate the above information. First, in 1840 two females in Reuben's household were born between 1816 and 1830 and another female was born between 1824 and 1830. This would suggest that there were three daughters rather than two. Second, in 1850, a Margaret Jones, age 21, born in VA, was living with Reuben. She was the right age for the youngest female in the 1840 household; thus, she was possibly the youngest daughter. Also in the 1850 household of Reuben Jones was Robert Love, age 25, born in VA, and Nancy Love, age two, born in OH. Martha and Margaret could have been the same person. John L. Jones did not name her in his discussion of her family in *The History of the Jones Family* but only noted she was the youngest daughter. In 1860 Robert Love, age 37, born in VA, was still living in Fayette Twp., Lawrence Co., OH (p. 28, *1860 Census*). He was head of the household. The remainder of the household was made up of M____ J., age 25, born in OH; Sally, age 13, born in OH; Mary, age 7, born in OH; Susanna Love, age 6, born in OH; Josephine, age 3, born in OH; and William, age 1, born in OH. It is possible that,

given possible errors made by the census taker and the difficulty in reading the very faint microfilm, M____ J. was Margaret/Martha Jones Love. No Fannie Lee or Robert are among the members of the household, but they could have been born after the 1860 census.]

18. Alexander[4] Jones. Born Sept 1851, OH, died ? He was a miner in Rendville, OH, ca. 1880. Married in Ft. Scott, KS, ca. 1890-1900. His wife, whose name is unknown, died in Ft. Scott after two children were born. Alexander returned home with his one surviving child. He became the pastor of his home church in Pomeroy, OH.

Issue: 33 i   daughter who died in infancy.
       34 ii Wert[5] Jones

20. John Lysandrous[4] Jones. Born 13 July 1857, Meigs Co., OH; died 13 May 1938, El Centro, CA. He was a miner in Rendville, OH, in 1881. Stayed in Rendville as a store owner and postmaster (appointed in 1897). He wrote *The History of the Jones Family* ca. 1928-1930. Married Sadie Broadis in 1884, the first black school teacher in Perry Co., OH, and the first school teacher of any race in Rendville. She died ca. 1930, and he moved to El Centro to be near his oldest child.

Issue: 35 i   Zenobia Broadis[5] Jones. Born in 1885 in Perry Co., OH; took the Boxwell Exam at age 12. Finished the N & I School at Institute, WV, in 1901. Attended Denison where she met and married W. A. Payne. They had eight children. The oldest daughter, Octavia, received a degree from the University of Southern California in June 1929 or 1930. Zenobia died after 1930, possibly, in El Centro, CA.

       36 ii Ethel Mae Jones. Born in 1889, Perry Co., OH. Attended West Virginia State College, University of Chicago, and Columbia. She taught at Wilberforce for three years, then married Yale law graduate, H. G. Tolliver, of New Haven, CT. He died in June 1927. Ethel remained in New Haven as a city official.

       37 iii Hazel Jones. Born and died ca. 1890.

| 38 | iv | John L. Jones, Jr. Born 8 Mar 1891, died 29 Jan 1927; married George/Georgia E. Haynes in Boley, OK, and had one daughter. |
| 39 | v | Earl R. Jones. Born 5 Mar 1893, served in the 351st Field Artillery, Battery, F in World War I. Married Viola Page and had three children. |

22. Fleming Bertram[4] Jones. Born 25 Feb 1862, Gallipolis, OH; died after 1930. Married Mayme Morris, a Middleport, OH, school teacher before 1897-1900. In 1884-1885 he took his brother John's new bride's position at the Rendville school, teaching there one year. He left to become principal at the school in Middleport, Meigs Co., OH. In 1897 he took his brother James McHenry's position in Wheeling, WV, when James became president of West Virginia State College. In 1909 his physician advised him to go west so he took his wife and two boys to Boley, OK. He and his wife joined the faculty of the Creek and Seminole University, he as acting president and she as music director. In 1910 he joined the staff of the Farmers' and Merchants Bank in Boley. In 1921 he helped form the First National Bank of Boley, the first national bank owned and operated by African-Americans.

| Issue: 40 | i | Lotis[5] Jones. Born ca. 1898-1900, probably in Wheeling, WV. He graduated high school in 1914 and did two years of pre-med at Langston University (Oklahoma State). He finished at Meharry Medical College in Nashville, TN, in 1924 and established a medical practice in Cleveland, OH, in 1925. He married Lyla C. Watson of Ardmore, OK, 4 Feb 1924 in Nashville. They had one child as of the writing of *The History of the Jones Family*: Lotis, Jr., born 12 Nov 1929. |
| 41. | ii | Claude B. Jones. Born ? He attended Wilberforce University and at the writing of his uncle's book was known as the "trombone king" with the Fletcher Henderson Orchestra. He married Alma Thomas, a co-ed at the University of Michigan in 1927. |

23. Charles⁴ Jones. Born 13 May 1865, Southpoint, Lawrence Co., OH; died 6 Aug 1928, probably Institute, WV. He is buried next to James McHenry Jones in Institute. He began his teaching career in Gallia Co., OH, and then took his brother Fleming's job in Rendville. He later joined the faculty at Institute. Married Mary F. Vance of Rendville, who died 16 months after Charles's death and is also buried in Institute.

Issue: 42   i   James McHenry⁵ Jones. Born in Rendville he graduated from West Virginia State College. After serving in World War I, he attended Meharry Medical College in Nashville. In 1930 he had a dental practice in Alton, IL.

43   ii   Bulah Jones. Born in Rendville; died young.

44   iii   Eunice Jones. Born in Rendville; died at 16, buried in Institute.

45   iv   Charles Connelly Jones. Born in Institute he finished the "normal course" there and attended Ohio University. He joined his brother at Meharry Medical College and was a dentist in Chicago in 1930.

46   v   Margaret Jones. Born in Institute, she and her sister, Eula Fay, received their college degrees the day after their father was buried. In 1930 she was teaching music at Institute.

47   vi   Eula Fay Jones. Born in Institute she was teaching in WV in 1930.

48   vii   Maurice Reid Jones. Born in Institute, he finished school in 1928 and became secretary to Capt. G.E. Ferguson, Director of Negro Welfare and Statistics.

49   viii Edward Francis Jones. Still in school in 1930.

50   ix   Louis Earl Jones. Still in school in 1930.

Undocumented Chart
by Eva L. Jones Slater
2 March 1983
showing possible interrelationships of the
Jones, Tanner & Bryant families

AFRICA - wed?
born 1744
|
Rueben Jones of Henrico County, VA - wed ?Ailstock, b. 1795

Issue:
John Jones ——— 12 children, daughter, Emma, wed Alfred Tanner
Joseph Jones ——— Boy, John, wrote History
Mary Francis Jones ——— born 1825, wed Flemmon Bryant
Martha Jones ——— 2 girls, Columbus, OH (what was husband's name?)

Emmanuel Tanner wed Eliza Tanner, both of Bedford County
|
Alfred Tanner, b. 1830 Bedford Co., wed Edith Haynes, b. 1842
|
Emma Jones wed Alfred Tanner
|
Mary E. Tanner wed James Bryant (below)

John Bryant of Rockingham County, VA

Issue:
Flemmon Bryant ——— born 1825 OH, wed Mary Francis Jones above
Wm. Bryant ——— born 1815 VA, father of I.V. Bryant (?)
Sarah Bryant ——— born 1826 OH
George Bryant ——— born 1817 VA

Flemmon Bryant, born 1825, wed Mary Francis Jones
|
James Bryant wed Mary E. Tanner (dau. of Emma Jones)
|
Clara Bryant wed Luke Beatty
|
Elsie Beatty wed Lawrence Jones (of the KY Joneses)
|
Eva L. Jones wed Mr. Slater

John L. Jones

HISTORY

of the

JONES FAMILY

by

John L. Jones
Rendville, Ohio

The Greenfield Printing & Publishing Company
Greenfield, Ohio

PREFACE

Few families belonging to our group know anything whatever about their people beyond the present generation. I have determined that this shall not be true of our family, so I have gathered all the data available and dedicated myself to the task of handing it down to our children and children's children yet to come. They have a right to know something of their background, something of the people from whom they sprang. Were they industrious, religious, intelligent, ignorant? Many such questions will arise which we hope to answer in this little history of the Jones family.

We have no motive other than to satisfy an urgent request by our children to leave them something reliable and definite concerning their people, as they believe that there are some things worth preserving. I do not expect to derive any benefit from the sale of this story, the expense of printing will be borne by me and by donation from members of the family.

Credit and thanks are due a nephew, Maurice Jones, who copied my manuscript, wrote the part pertaining to his sister Eunice (deceased) and made helpful suggestions.

DEDICATION

This Story is Lovingly
Dedicated to my Wife
Who Has Been My
Inspiration for Forty-
five Years . . . . .

The Story of the Jones Family

by John L. Jones

In the year 1754, a ship with a cargo of African slaves landed at Jamestown, Virginia, among them was a boy 10 years of age, a son of an African prince. This boy became the father of the family of whom we write, a family now scattered throughout many states of the Union. Most Negroes brought to this country at this time were sold to planters for slaves to work for them without compensation, and there was no law to prevent it. These people were considered as chattel and sold to the highest bidder. They were induced to come aboard the ship by lying lips promising many impossible things, some were forced aboard and when they found their awful plight, many of them cast themselves into the sea, finding watery graves rather than submit to slavery.

This boy grew to manhood without having to submit to the yoke of bondage. The only reason that can be assigned is that they had respect for the royal blood that was known to course through his veins. This may or may not be true but this we know, that he nor none of his posterity were ever held as slaves.[1]

In the course of time he married. Of his wife we know but little, but this we know to a certainty that his wife was a free woman, else her children would have been slaves. Children of free parents could not be enslaved according to the law then prevailing, especially if the mother was a free woman, neither could the children of a white mother be enslaved even though the father was a Negro.

There were many cases of this kind all through these slave-holding states which account for so many free Negroes. I do not know the number of children born to this first family. My father told us the story more than once, but I cannot say with certainty as to his uncles, he spoke more often of his father who was a son of this pair and whose name was Reuben Jones.

Reuben Jones was born in Henrico County, Virginia, in 1795. We can say but little of his life from birth to manhood. While he was free born and could go and come at will he could not go to any school. Negro children were not allowed to handle a book and it was a crime to teach them to read or write. The ruling class knew very well that the best way to keep the Negro in submission was to keep him in ignorance. They knew that if they would allow the Negro, even the free Negro, the privilege of learning that he would teach the slaves also. While they argued that the Negroes' head was thick and that he could not learn they ruthlessly and brutally withheld from Reuben Jones the opportunity to learn even his alphabet.

Coming to maturity he began to cast about for a life companion, that was a hard proposition when we consider the surroundings. There were many slaves who would be desirable but the children, if any, would be slaves. Coming up in a slave community and seeing the way slaves were treated and cuffed about, a girl from this class could not be considered.

There was in this neighborhood a family by the name of Ailstock, the father was an Englishman, the mother was an Indian Squaw. Besides father and mother there were three girls, two of whom were white, taking their complexion from their father, the other girl was of a little darker hue. The two white ones married white men and were lost in the white race. The girl of darker hue married Reuben Jones. These sisters went in opposite directions and never met each other again.[2]

Reuben Jones was not a stranger to work, that was all there was for a poor Negro boy to do. He worked for the farmers round about him and had saved his earnings preparatory for the change that is now upon him. His first thought was a home, that is the dream of every wide-awake young man. He bought a home that is a tract of land, wood land, and set about to build a home. He soon cleared a place large enough for his house and in a short while his house was finished and they moved in.

To provide for a family now coming on, to discharge the notes on his place as they became due, was his problem, up to this time he had found a way, from this time on, he must make a way.

During this period of our history, coal, coal oil, gas, and electricity were unknown. Wood only was used for all domestic purposes. By this time Reuben Jones had felled trees, mauled rails, built fences, grubbed out underbrush and had a part of his place ready for cultivation.

Reuben Jones and wife were Christians, the wife was loved and respected for her devoted life and Christian integrity. They had four children, John, Joseph, Mary and Martha. They must have had some knowledge of the Bible, else whence these names? The colored people of this community had a church of some description of which Reuben and wife were members. I have often heard my father tell of the time that he, when a small boy, was refused membership in the church because when giving in his experience, he did not see the devil, nor hear chains rattle, neither did he go to the graveyard to pray at midnight. That was enough. He was sent back and told that he did not have the genuine religion.

These boys were put to work at an early age. At 10, Joseph was given a team, he made a round trip to Richmond every day with a load of cord-wood—a distance of 10 miles. Wood was in great demand and the only fuel available for domestic purposes. This wood was sold for cash and the proceeds turned over to the father every night less three cents, the liberal allowance given the boy for lunch. The lunch consisted of bread 1¢, molasses 2¢. After finishing this splendid repast he would start on his return trip for home.

The roads were mud roads, at times almost impassable. Some nights he would not reach home until midnight. One night he went to sleep. The horses pulled off to the side of the road and stopped. When he awoke the day was breaking, fortunately he was not far from home. He reached home in time for breakfast and after finishing breakfast he started again his daily grind. This treatment was too much for the mother and she entered a protest, but to no avail. It seemed that Joseph was his mother's favorite, while John was his father's. John was the picture of his father, while Joseph was in disposition and facial appearance that of his mother.

Joseph had many advantages over his brother. In his daily trips to Richmond he had contact with people and in that way learned among other things the way to complete freedom, through this contact he figured out his way to Ohio. With the approval of his mother and the kindly advice of friends he gathered together his belongings, wrapped them up in a red bandanna handkerchief and in the quiet of the night he silently stole away.

This journey for a boy just 13 was not without hazard. The distance to Ohio was about 400 miles through an unbroken country, and at that time the mountains were said to have wild beasts in plenty. Again he was traveling without free papers, he either forgot them or did not know that they were necessary. All free Negroes could get free papers from the county court house with the county seal affixed, so in case of question they could show their papers and pass on, otherwise they could be arrested by any white man and sold into slavery. He made his escape and finally landed on the bank of the Kanawha River near Point Pleasant in sight of the state of Ohio, his objective. While standing there a steamboat came down the river, he waved at the boat. The captain took it for a signal to land, bringing his boat to land he asked the boy what he wanted. To which he replied, "Do you need any men on this boat?" The captain ordered the stage plank lowered, and the boy went aboard. This boat was bound for Cincinnati, Ohio, with this new boy, working at a new job in a new world.[3]

A steamboat crew is not complete without a deck sweep. There happened to be none on this boat at this time, being too light to handle heavy freight, he was given the job of deck sweep. The pay of the deck sweep was some less than that of the deck hands.

His first night on the boat was one of fear and terror. The patter of the wheels, the noise of the engines, the singing of the laborers, swearing, gambling, everything different and opposite from what he expected. His bed was a box, a board, a pile of freight of any description and sometimes the bare floors. There was no provision made for the comfort of the men on the lower deck.

As he could not sleep he had all night for reflection, time to ruminate and ponder over his past, and time also to contrast the home given up for the life that he is now entering into. All through this long night his dear loving mother stood beside him, his father who was so exacting and cause of his plight was in their midst. Brother John, Mary and Martha were sad and lonesome without him, weeping and longing for his return. This boy is not having his trouble alone, the whole family is upset, not knowing that he, like the Joseph for whom he is named, will later become the savior of the family. Early the next morning the boat reached Cincinnati, Ohio, metropolis of the West and gateway to the South, the largest port between New Orleans and Pittsburg, Pennsylvania. Here the largest boats afloat discharged their cargoes for distribution east and west, here people of every race assembled to share in the common labor loading and unloading these boats, the wharf is strewn with women, there to share in the pay of their husbands and sweethearts. A strange panorama is passing before this boy from the woods of Virginia.

After the boat was made fast to the wharf the crew made a mad rush far up town where they will put in their time among the worst element in the city—among the saloon element and tents of wickedness. They could not induce Joseph to go with them, he preferred to stay aboard the boat. This gave the captain and mate an opportunity to question him. They learned from him that he could neither read nor write, and expressed to them his desire to learn. The good captain secured the necessary books and a slate and gave him his first lesson before leaving Cincinnati on their return trip.

These trips were kept up from August to December and after these months he had never left the boat, had never gone up the bank. As soon as his work was done he began his studies. I have heard him say often that he never got lonesome, that he was so hungry for knowledge that he did not want to be disturbed, no one except his teacher could entertain him. He knew that he was not in a position to associate with the best people and would not associate with that lower element who frequented those places of sin and vice. This was the last trip for two months, the mercury fell on this night 10 degrees below zero. The next morning there was a heavy flow of ice in the river.

Later the river was frozen solid from shore to shore. Seeing the condition of the river and no prospect of a break for at least two months the hands were called to the office and paid off. These men, about fifty in all, must make their way home as best they can, or lie around Cincinnati and wait for the February thaw. The good captain told his scholar that he could stay on the boat with him and that his pay would remain the same. Surely goodness and mercy followed him, else what would have become of this inexperienced homeless boy?

At the end of his term, three years, with this master he could read and write, and was advanced far enough in arithmetic to take care of his accounts, that is, he had mastered the four fundamentals and that was considered a good education in that day. He learned in the meantime to read music, and afterward became an instructor in vocal music.

Music to him was a gift from Heaven, and while he was blessed with this talent a beautiful voice was thrown in, a voice sonorous and vibrating, charming, soft and clear. Here is one of his favorite sayings: "'Tis not enough the voice be sound and clear, 'tis modulation that must charm the ear." He had a well-modulated voice. We read about Dunbar's Malinda, but you ought to have heard Joseph sing. I have never heard a man who could approximate him.

Tired of boating for a while, having saved a considerable sum of money, he went to Cincinnati, built up his wardrobe, secured a boarding place, also a place to work. His first job was gouger in a flour barrel coopershop. The wages were small but sufficient to keep down his expenses until he could learn the trade. After establishing himself in his new home and under these changed environments he began attending church. The Baptist church was the only church that he had ever attended, the church of his parents the one in which he was refused admission, yet the one he loved. A Reverend Shelton was pastor of the Baptists at this time and they had purchased a fine edifice from a Jewish congregation. Attracted by this fine place of worship together with his anxiety to be of service he presented himself for membership and was accepted without question. It was not a hard matter for him to weave himself into the good graces of the congregation, he was well dressed, neat, and clean in speech as well as personal appearance, a strictly religious young man with a good easy flow of the English language. In that day the singing was by the congregation. The preacher would line out a hymn and someone in the congregation would pitch it and lead it through. One morning the preacher lined out a common particular meter, and none of the members could sing it, so Joseph was glad of the opportunity to step forward and show them how to sing a common particular meter. From that morning he became the leader of the congregational singing.

Learning that he was proficient in vocal music they asked him to organize a choir. He did not organize a church choir but organized a singing school and invited anyone who wanted to be instructed in the science of vocal music. He carried on this school until he had developed among the young people a number of good singers and ready readers at which time he organized and became the chorister of the choir. The church was, in this day, the community center for the people of our race, all of our religious and social activities were centered there. We had no part in the political or civic affairs of the city. This brought him in contact with the cream of society which had been his dream from the day he left home until the present.

After learning his trade and working for sometime on a berth alone, the coopers were laid off for a while, as in this day the supply was greater than the demand, so Joseph went into the whitewash and calcimine business, and finding this lucrative, continued until at about twenty when he felt the call for the old steamboat life again. He had a longing to see his old friends, the old scenes along the shore of the beautiful Ohio, the towering hills, the wide valleys, the great hanging rocks, tasseling corn and waving wheat fields, the noise of the engine and sound of the wheels that at first annoyed but is now sweet music to his ears. Then he longed to visit the old towns again, Portsmouth, Gallipolis, Point Pleasant, Pomeroy, New Richmond, Ripley, Burlington, Southpoint, and others of less importance. At Southpoint a young lady came out on the bank and waved at her uncle, and Joseph asked him her name, he told him, and added that if he wanted to meet her that he would take him with him the next time he went home. Some weeks after this he went to Southpoint with her Uncle George Bryant, who was second engineer on this boat. They met, he wooed her and in about a year after, they wed. The name of this girl was Temperance Reed. She was born in Burlington, Ohio, May 15, 1824. Her parents were William and Nancy Reed who came to this state many years before this incident.[4]

This girl was the oldest of a family of eight children who were classed among the best people of Southern Ohio. They were Christians and one, Samuel Reed, was a preacher, William was an engineer, James and George were barbers, John was a boatman. Mary married Belfield Johnson and Rosetta married Ambrose Smith, both being prosperous farmers. These farms are being operated today by their children and grandchildren. This girl was reared by a rich family in Southpoint and what education she had was through the kindness of this family, as no provision was made in Ohio at this early date for the education of colored children.

Father Reed owned and operated a farm in this section on what is called Solidy. Both died there.

Joseph and Temperance Jones spent their honeymoon at the home of the latter's parents and other friends in the community. Most of the people around Burlington and Southpoint, in fact through the country, were related to Mrs. Jones. They came from near and far to see this big catch by their favorite cousin, this well-dressed and rather versatile young man from the big city.

Time rolled on while Joseph left for Gallipolis where he intended to begin housekeeping. He secured a house, furnished it and brought his bride and started on their life journey.

The next thing was a job, not a position but a job. Positions were for the white man and not a Negro. A colored man was satisfied with a job. He knew that he could steamboat and that there was always a job waiting for him there, he could whitewash and calcimine and was a good cooper so he applied for a job in Langley's cooper shop. Securing the job for which he applied, he set about on life's next lap.

The people of Gallipolis had two very good churches and were well attended. Both being of the Baptist faith Joseph and his wife at once joined that church. The church edifice was not to be compared with the big Jewish church in Cincinnati, but it was a place of worship, and they at once entered into work. Joseph organized his singing school and a house-to-house singing club composed of the young married people of their set. Temperance fell in with this arrangement as she had a beautiful voice but knew nothing whatever about vocal music. She had a natural alto voice while Joseph would alternate between bass and tenor as the case would require. Other families belonging to this class were the Wards, Masons, Vineys, Thompsons, Gees, Holmes and others. Young and old attended church, some because they loved the service and others because they had no other place to go. Such things as Sunday movies, Sunday baseball, Sunday dog racing were unknown.

Eleven years had passed since Joseph quit the state of Virginia, and came to the state of Ohio. What has happened to his family in all of these years he had not the faintest idea, and what had become of him was equally remote. If any of them could write they would not know where to address their letters. If he should write to them they would not get his letter as they never go to the post office and never received a letter. The nearest post office is Richmond—10 miles away—and he felt certain that to write them would be a waste of time.

Being ardent Christians they had established the family altar in their home, and prayed earnestly for the God of all power to bring the family together again. Trusting in him and believing implicitly in the efficacy of prayer they decided to wait on the Lord.

The birth of William Henry, their first child, is announced, named for William Henry Harrison who was president at the time of their marriage. Differing from his father by taking his name from history while his father selected his names from the Bible.

A full year had passed since he came to Gallipolis. Work was plentiful and he had managed to save a good part of his earnings, due in large part to the economy of his good wife who insisted on clipping a margin from each dollar coming into the house.

Joseph Jones was a man of large ideas. He was in a position to buy and pay for a small house and was advised to do so by his wife, but had his idea about the kind of a home he wanted and it was that kind or none until he could make himself able to carry out his large ideas. He had his eye on a double lot situated in a part of the city in which he desired to live. This lot faced on two streets, on the corner lot he wanted to build a business building, next to this a dwelling house and farther around on the next street a cooper shop. His pardonable pride would not allow him to think of doing small things. He was looked upon as one of the leaders in church and his advice was sought in matters pertaining to civic affairs, and must live in a style becoming his standing.

The work had closed down again and Joseph must choose between loafing around town for a season or going back to the river, after resting for one week he decided to try the river again. When single he rather enjoyed the change from land to water, but since he had a family he preferred home. All through his life he carried out this idea, never wait for a job. When one gives out, go after another one.

He was known as a good boatman and never experienced any difficulty in securing a good job there. He secured a place as watchman on this boat and remained away for six months leaving with his wife a relative, Sarah Bryant. Sarah Bryant was a young woman and aunt of Temperance. In September, 1851, Alexander, the second son was born, the father came home for a few days and after becoming acquainted with his big boy and making the necessary arrangements for the family, he returned to the boat again. Few men of his race kept closer to current affairs. He was a constant reader and was posted on the doings of Congress. Through this period there was much feeling against the Negro, while at the same time there were many friends coming to his aid both in and out of Congress. Charles Summer had recently been elected to the Senate from Massachusetts. Abraham Lincoln was coming to the front. The lightning was flashing in the distance, the clouds looked menacing and the thunder was roaring. To him this meant that God was ruling and that good would come out of it all.

The opportunity came for work at home making flour barrels for Ailshire's mill, and he bade farewell to steamboating forever. His oldest boys were getting old enough to go to school and as there was no school for colored boys he went to other families of the race and got their consent to organize a pay school. They secured enough scholars and hired Mr. Joe Ward to teach. The school house was the Baptist church. This was the first school for colored children in Gallipolis. When William Henry was six years old he could read in the third reader, and could work arithmetic as far as division.

Old people were amazed and could hardly believe what they would see and hear, they told the family that they would never raise him, they laughed at what they called fogyism. But he died in his eighth year. The third boy, Josephus, born in 1854, was then about one year old. Aunt Sarah Bryant was still living with them. A young man is going with her—name withheld for reasons—they tarried at the gate too long for Joseph. One night after coming from church, he went out and told them to either come in the house or go home. This incensed the young man and he went away breathing out threats. The next evening he met Joseph about a square from his home and made a rush at him with a drawn dagger. Joseph retreated and gained enough distance to snatch a picket off the fence and when his enemy was in striking distance he struck him down, depriving him of his dagger, and flogged him plenty. The doctors dressed his wounds and within three weeks he was out but never called on Aunt "Sary" again.

Joseph was a powerful man and too proud to fight only when imposed upon. In that day it was almost impossible to keep out of a fight. Fighting seemed to be in the air, his fights were always on the defensive.

In Pomeroy, Ohio, there was a great demand for coopers, the wages were inviting, so Joseph moved there and engaged in that work for a while. Moving was simple and easy in those days and not to be compared with moving of today. They had no pianos, kitchen cabinets, sideboards, radios, bookcases, Victorolas, davenports, mattresses, etc., just a few pieces of furniture, such as one two-hole stove, a bed (the children slept on the floor), one rag carpet, bedding, and a few kitchen utensils, and dishes.

July 13, 1857, another little boy with a big name came into the world and to this family; I speak of John Lysandrous. I refer to the writer of this book. This name was given to me by my father for no other reason than his being famed for big names. I have searched ancient history and encyclopedias through and through and cannot find that name and think my father must have gotten the name confused with Lycurgus, a Spartan general, and as I don't like either of the names, discarded them years ago and write my name John L. Jones.[5] The temporary sojourn to Pomeroy was soon ended, and the family returned to Gallipolis by the way of Cincinnati. The first move after reaching Gallipolis was the purchase of the coveted double lot cited several years before. A five-room brick house was erected on the lot next to the corner while the corner lot was reserved for a business building. To the house was built a large porch extending across the front and leading back to the door entering the dining room. The building sat about twenty feet back and a beautiful grassy yard gave the house a splendid setting. As soon as the house was completed the family moved in their new home, using the old furniture with the addition of a few new pieces. The home was completed, the next move is a building on the corner lot. The contract was let and a frame business structure was soon erected. A cooper shop was built on the lot facing on another street. Hoop poles, staves, heading and all necessary material were purchased. Coopers were hired and set to work making flour barrels for Joseph Jones. These barrels were sold on a contract with the two large flour mills then working at full capacity in the town.

He acted as foreman until one of his men was trained in the business of buying and selecting timber, then the shop was turned over to him. Joseph bought a team of horses and a light wagon and went into the huckster business, using the building on the corner for storage of butter, eggs, chickens, fruit of all kinds. On Saturdays he would stay at home and run off the overflow. While the business proved profitable it will be seen later that it was only a blind to cover up another business on which his heart was fixed. The people on the little farm near Richmond had at last learned of Joseph's whereabouts. Brother John sold the farm and came to Ohio, bringing his parents and sisters with him. They landed at Gallipolis and were directed to the home of their son and brother. They were received midst tears and laughter, Grandmother Jones resting on the breast of her favorite son wept copiously. Many a Hallelujah and Praise God went up from the lips of all. This was the answer to twenty years of prayer, this was the faith that believes in waiting on the Lord.[6]

Father and Mother Jones were old and broken in health, they had never known anything but hard work, for years they had been incapacitated and all fell on brother John. So Joseph was glad to be in a position to take his father and mother and keep them for the remainder of their days. So far as the money from the sale of the home is concerned, take it and use it to give yourself and the girls a start in life. I will look after mother and father to the end. After visiting with his brother for several weeks, John went to Ross County and bought a farm. Land was cheap at that time, not over 15¢ or 20¢ per acre. He raised two sets of children and became well-to-do. His farm consisting of 240 acres is still in the hands of his children. The relationship between the brothers was very cordial, yet they never visited each other often. Uncle John was at our house once while we lived in Pomeroy, he drove through with two fine iron grays. I think the prettiest matches that I ever saw were his when he came to our house. That was the only time that any of us saw Uncle John. Oteria, a lovely daughter, stayed with us one winter and went to school. This was the only one of the children that any of our family ever met until a few years ago.

John Jones was the father of 12 children in the following order: Joseph Jones, Civil War soldier; Octavia; Oteria, school teacher; Emma; William, farmer; Elizabeth Hill, 6 children, 3 of her sons are among the foremost mechanics in the city of Columbus, Ohio; Sylvanis, farmer; Edward, cement contractor and bricklayer; Reuben, engineer and teacher; George, undertaker; Maria, teacher; Marshall, the father of 10 children, died recently. The farm consisting of 240 acres is now in possession of his widow. This is the old home place located in Jackson County, Ohio. Aunt Mary Bryant had five children: Charles, house mover and contractor; Abraham; Joseph, one-time member of the Columbus police force; and Flem and James; all of this family are dead. Charlie Bryant, Jr., of Columbus, the son of the late Charley Bryant, is one of the leading business men of the race, besides being a contractor and house mover he has six gas stations, held blocks of stock in several financial institutions and operated one of our leading hotels. The youngest sister had two children, Fannie Lee and Robert Love. Fannie died in Columbus, Ohio, a few years ago.[7]

Of the 12 children of John Jones's family only two are living. Of the 10 children of Joseph Jones's family, two are living. All of the other two families are dead. This is one of the largest families in the state of Ohio, and we take pride in stating that from our great grandfather down to the present we have not produced a physical, mental or moral incompetent. Those who have passed on were intelligent, outstanding characters and those of the present are desirable citizens in their several communities.

James Henry was born August 30th, 1859, a few months before John Brown seized the arsenal at Harper's Ferry, Virginia.[8] This master stroke by this great man sent chills up the spine of the people of North and South. It threw many into spasms while many more laughed at the ignorance of the old man, but as silly as it might have seemed, it started something that the wise ones did not know how to start. The sound that was made soon spread over the country and the next year nominated and elected Abraham Lincoln president of the United States of America. John Brown was the best friend the Negro ever had. He did in a few hours what others wanted to do but lacked the nerve. He loved the Negro and chanced his life for their freedom. They called him crazy and thought that the trouble was over when they hung him to a tree, but as the poet sang, "Brown, Brown O sweet o my Brown, he'll trouble you more than ever when you've nailed his coffin down." Joseph's father died in this year, notwithstanding the love and tenderness with which he was surrounded, he could never quite give up the old home. The nice brick house in Gallipolis, could not take the place of the hewed log house on his own place. He worried quite a bit also on account of his wife who was ill at this time. Joseph quit the huckster business for a time and stayed at home to attend to his parents and as he promised his brother to stick to them to the last, he carried out his promise. Both died in this year and were buried at Macadonia, Lawrence County, Ohio.[9]

Let it be known here that from the time his parents landed in Ohio to the time of their death and burial did he allow anyone to share in any expense connected with them. Friends of the slaves had by this time established the Underground Railway, an organization to assist the slave to escape from slavery to freedom. If a runaway slave could reach the Ohio River the Railway would assist him through the states of Ohio and Indiana to Canada where he would be free. Before this road was established many slaves were caught by their pursuers and returned to their owners. The fugitive slave law allowed the master to pursue his slaves and return them from any state in the Union, but if they could get through the states and place their feet on English soil they were forever free.

This Railway established stations along the line and a conductor, called an Underground Railway conductor, at every station. Some of these conductors were white and some colored.

Joseph Jones was the conductor for the Gallipolis station. The store room on the corner was built with this in view. In this building was an especially prepared room to feed and house the fugitives. These men hired by the master class were desperate characters and went heavily armed, so also did the conductors. Joseph never left home without his two ominous-looking guns about 18 inches long. There was no chance to take possession of his men without first killing him. No one ever suspected that he was interested in this traffic. These people were brought to him at night, and left at night. If suspicious characters were noticed loitering around, they were kept in hiding until the opportunity came to run them off to the next station. It was known that a station was located in Gallipolis, but they never succeeded in finding it. He always left at night with his load of human freight and returned with his load of produce, thus playing double, keeping down suspicion.[10]

Albany, Ohio, was the next station, from where they were smuggled through to Deavertown, Morgan County, Tommy Gray was the conductor for that station. He was a white man of the John Brown type. In later years the writer had him come to Rendville, Ohio, to make a speech on Emancipation Day. He was the same friend to the Negro that he was in the sixties. At another time I visited his home, he told of a little experience he had with three slaves while taking them to the Zanesville station. He had a load of potatoes and three men in his wagon. It had been raining the night before and the road was slippery. He came to a hill and his horses could not pull the wagon up the hill. Just at that time two men came down the hill riding two fine horses, they had been to Zanesville, on the track of the men he had in his wagon. The men were covered over with quilts just as the potatoes were, and the riders did not suspect that the slaves they were hunting were in the wagon. Mr. Gray asked them to help him up the hill, so they hitched their horses to his wagon and pulled his load and their load up the hill. Tommy knew who they were and knew their mission, but made this play so as to allay any suspicion harbored in their minds.

Zanesville was considered the hardest town in the state to pass through. There were Knights of the Golden Circle, Butternuts, and other organizations in sympathy with the South and antipathetic to the Negro. If they could pass through Zanesville, they had little or no trouble to reach the lakes, thence to Canada. On February 25th, 1862, the seventh son, Fleming Bertram Jones was born. The Civil War was now in full force and slaves coming to Ohio were undisturbed and unmolested. It would be very unhealthy for anyone to say that he was on the hunt for slaves to turn them back to their masters. He would be mobbed on the spot. There was no more use for the Underground Railway, it had done the work well and surrendered to a higher power. The huckster business passed with the Railway, and Joseph went into the business of delivering freight to the stores from the wharf. Tom Holmes looked after the freight while he continued at his trade.

The citizens of Gallipolis were good people as a whole, and would average with the people of other border towns along the Ohio River. There were, on the other hand, many of the worst sort floating in who were not of value to the city. Their influence with the younger set to which my brothers belonged was disturbing to my parents, and the question arose: what shall we do?

The war was now on in full force, not only at the front, but on the streets everywhere. Bill Wright, the town bully, came to the shop one day and began to abuse my father, cursed him and used all the vile and nasty language that he could think of, and dared him to come out of the shop. Father went out of the back door to his home. Wright went around the corner and stood at the gate, keeping up the same language and begging him to come out so that he could mop the ground with him. Mother begged him not to go out, but Wright kept up such a tirade of abuse, Father could not stand it any longer. He walked down and opened the gate, started across the street, the street was very muddy and boards were laid across to keep people out of the mud. Wright followed him to the middle where Father wheeled around and struck him between the eyes, knocking him down into the mud. Wright jumped up, waving his arms and shouting, "I am a man!" He made another pass at Father, and at the same time received another blow in the same place with the same result. He came back the third time and the result was the same. That was sufficient. The man was as muddy as a hog coming from his wallow. This was the first fight that I ever saw. I was a very small boy and had heard of the war and wondered why they did not send my father to the front. He would end it all in a short while.

Around this corner a lot of soldiers from camp just outside the town limits, assembled one day. The commander was out of town, the soldiers were drinking and making a general disturbance. A colored woman came by and one of the soldiers for some cause slapped her. A certain colored man standing by shot the soldier and ran for his life. It was all done so quick that they did not see who did the shooting. The soldiers with gun and bayonet searched every Negro home in town for him and pursued him as far as Albany. They ate dinner with him the next day in a hotel but did not know him. That night, because of the feeling against the colored people, the men thought it best to take their families out of town. Father took us away out somewhere but he came back to the house as did many of the men who had removed their families to safety.

The Joneses and their set were very dressy in those days. Their clothes would put to shame some of the $22.50 suits of the present day. I can remember the suit my father wore when I was a boy of five. His boots were shop made, suit was black English broadcloth, silk plug hat, white shirt with pleated bosom about ½-inch wide, low-cut vest so as to show stud pin in shirt, white collar, black bow tie. In winter a heavy shawl was worn instead of an overcoat, folded so as to hang down at a point before and behind, instead of buttons, two large gold pins were used. My mother was a seamstress, and made her own clothes. Her clothes were of the best quality. I remember a black silk dress that she had for extraordinary occasions, she kept the dress from the time I was a little boy until I became a man. When the style would change she would alter the dress to suit, she was so careful with it that after twenty years of occasional use it was still in good condition.

Shawls were in use by women also, or rather two shawls, one a little breakfast shawl to keep the shoulders warm and a larger one of beautiful color and design. She was modest in dress although always appeared well. Father being semi-professional, she was more interested in him, and looked after him to the minutest detail.

Besides making their own clothes, women of that day knit the stockings for the family, when calling they would take their yarn and knitting needles and talk while knitting, often finishing a sock while visiting. I never saw any cards in our house, I presume they knew nothing about bridge. The war is waxing hot. Lightburn is on retreat down the Kanawha Valley, bringing with him thousands of refugees. Among them a flat boat of slaves fleeing to a place of safety, they landed at the wharf at Gallipolis. I was on the dray with Tom Holmes, the man who worked for my father. These people laughed, cried and shouted for hours. I have never seen people so happy as they were, some of them would get down and kiss the ground. They were dressed in all kinds of funny clothes, but they were clean. The home men knew nothing of their coming, and were at sea as to shelter and food. Finally they got together and secured the two churches until they could make permanent arrangements.

They remained several days in the churches before places were found for them. They sang and rejoiced night and day, the people of the town were about as happy as they were. Joseph Jones and his set were active in finding places for them by canvassing the town among white and black, all were responsive to their appeals, and in a short while, homes were found for all.

I shall never forget Aunt Nelly, one of the women who stayed with my mother. We became good friends, and understood each other perfectly. I would pick up stumps of cigars for her to smoke in her pipe. She would, in turn, spread me a big fat piece of bread with butter and sugar on it. Besides her kindness to me she was lovely to every one. I have never been able to locate her as the only name that I knew was Aunt Nelly. She and Mother were the best of friends, and when she left, the parting was very sad.

Everything was happening in Gallipolis those days, and it was not a very desirable place in which to live. Near our home there was a saloon, the soldiers from the convalescent hospital frequented it. One of them called up the drinks and was kicked out of the place because he had no money to pay for them. He told the big red-faced saloon keeper that he was going to the hospital and get his gun and come back and kill him. This saloon man was a rebel sympathizer and these soldiers knew it and were anxious to have a reason for killing him. They went back to the camp and in about ten minutes they came back again. The saloon keeper was on the porch in front of his place reading a newspaper. The same three men returned, but only one had a gun. He rested the gun on the corner of our fence and shot. The man fell off his chair and was dead before anyone could reach him. This was the first man that I ever saw killed, and up to now, the last one.

My mother and brother, Josephus, were called as witnesses at the trial. The soldier was proven insane and that was the last of it.

Following this, another tragedy occurred. On the Public Well Corner during a drinking and gambling night of terror the gang beat and bruised a man by name, Summers Moss, and after robbing him carried him to the river bank and threw him over for dead. He lay there for the remainder of the night. The authorities found him the next morning, and finding a little life yet remaining they brought him back after taking seven bones out of his head. This was just one of many instances of this kind around this corner. Shortly after this the white and colored boys had a pitched battle in the street. Alex Jones struck a white boy on the head with a gavel, fracturing his skull. This created quite an excitement. Father had to spirit the boy away and keep him in hiding until it was certain that the boy would recover. These were strenuous times.[11]

Do you blame my parents for deciding to move their boys out of this environment? We can name a score of young men from every town along the Ohio River who went out in the world and made good in law, medicine, and in the profession of teaching, in the ministry, at business and along many other lines. And despite these unfavorable conditions the boys and girls of Gallipolis, we are proud to note, have made their contributions to the trades, to business and to the professions.

After years of pleasant association with the people of Gallipolis, Joseph Jones disposed of his holdings to good advantage, and with reluctance moved his family to near Southpoint, Lawrence County, Ohio. Here he rents what is known as the Church farm, one of the best river bottom farms of that section. He converted one of the buildings on the place into a shop and made barrels for a flouring mill in Ironton, Ohio, ten miles south. A hired man looked after the farm while he looked after the shop. For some time they had been receiving colored men in the war and he presented himself three times for enlistment and was turned down each time because of a small growth on his breast. It was innocent, but nevertheless they would not receive him. When a call came for volunteers he was active in making up the quota. On account of his activities he was spotted by the Butternuts, or men in the neighborhood in sympathy with the South. These Southern sympathizers uttered threats against my father at the time and Mother begged him to give up his activities, but since they would not receive him in the army he felt that he should do something to advance the cause. The thirteen years that he lived in Virginia gave him a vague idea of slavery, and he was willing to sacrifice his life if need be for the cause of freedom. Mother had a constant fear of these men coming in some night and doing bodily harm to the family but Father was determined to carry on.

One morning while we were at breakfast, three men riding large black horses rode up to the fence opposite our house. After making their horses fast they came straight to our door and made a mad rush toward Father who ran out a side door, the three red rebels in hot pursuit. Father gained enough on them to reach the shop, about 30 yards away, in time to fortify himself with a butt end of a hoop pole about three feet long and three inches in diameter. As they came to the door he would knock them down, if one would attempt to get up he would knock him down again. When he finished they were as bloody as hogs and so weak that they could make their way back to their horses only with difficulty. We lived in this place for three years after this incident. Father continued his activities in recruiting men for the war, but never had any more interference by the Butternuts.

I don't believe the country ever saw a darker period than the one just at the close of the Civil War. Especially as concerning the Negro. The only thing that kept him from despair was hope. When the blackest clouds overhung his head and thick darkness surrounded him everywhere eternal hope would spring up in his soul and a soft voice would whisper in his ear, it will be better farther on.

There was no thought of opening schools in this country for colored youths, our oldest boy was now about 14 with four more following, all to grow into manhood without education. This is nauseous to parents who live for their children and are so anxious for their future welfare. It will come, the break was sure to come, it was in the offing, but would it come in time for my boys to benefit? We hoped and trusted and prayed.

While living in this place cholera broke out. It was severe especially in Cincinnati. Father, having satisfied himself that he was not cut out for a farmer, went back to the city to engage in one of his old trades. While the cholera was raging, my mother saw an announcement in the paper of the death of Joseph Jones. You can imagine the anguish of the souls on the part of my mother, far out in the country, surrounded by hostile whites, five children and no friends for council or advice and husband and father lying in a morgue.

We were not in a suffering condition, we had cows, horses, some money and plenty of food, but what would this amount to with the breadwinner gone? This suspense lasted two or three days to be broken by Father appearing on the scene one morning about breakfast time. This was a morning of supreme joy. I never saw my father looking better, he seemed to have plenty of money. The trouble was over as far as the children were concerned when he threw a handful of small coins on the floor to have us scramble for them. Growing tired of these vicissitudes, these sporadic changes, he thought that he had found a place to settle down and give his boys a chance to go to school.

While at Cincinnati, he made a visit to New Richmond, Ohio, a town about twenty miles north, and after looking the place over, concluded to move his family there. This would be his first opportunity to place his boys in a public school. Within a few weeks we were living in New Richmond, a beautiful town of about three thousand inhabitants. There we found two good churches, both new and well attended, a very good school for that day and time. Best of all, the people were clean, intelligent, religious and very sociable. Father's work here was making tight barrels. These barrels were used for water, whiskey, oil or any liquids. As few coopers could make these barrels, the wages were above the average. The good wages enabled him to keep us in school. During the winter, we took advantage of this opportunity and studied night and day, each seemed to have a goal. The possibilities of the future had been drilled into us by our parents who had a vision of the future. We were taught that avenues now closed to us would be opened and now was the time to prepare for them. We were taught also that to educate the head and neglect the education of the heart should be unthinkable, they make good companions and should travel along together. We get knowledge by close and constant application to books, but wisdom comes from God. Be sure to mix a high moral character with your education and it is certain that you will end well.

Most of the men and boys in this town were boatmen when the stage of water would permit.Few of them worked on the deck, they were cooks, stewards, porters, cabin boys and musicians. Our boys were not allowed to steamboat or work in a barber shop. Father was opposed to any kind of labor that savored of the servant, he had seen too much of this in early life. He would rather have them dig in a ditch than fawn and grin for a tip. He was high minded, perhaps a little too much so, but it was inborn and he seemed to be satisfied with his spirit of respectful independence. May 13, 1865, Charles Jones was born in Southpoint just before the family moved to New Richmond. The family had now increased to eight in all and no one at work but Father. Alex, the oldest, found employment with a tobacco factory, while Josephus and John found odd jobs around the town. By school time they had earned enough to buy their clothes and books for the season. The boys belonging to my older brother's class were coming back from a trip on the river, looking rather starchy with their nice store clothes. The contrast was more than the boys could stand. The girls were attracted to these boatmen and at festivals and parties they were the rage, while our boys with their home-made clothes must stand back. Then again, the boys had some money to rattle in their pockets while our boys were contributing their little earnings to the family exchequer. Alex and Josephus were yet in their teens but considered themselves young men, and against their mother's protest (Father was out of town), took off with the boys to the boat.

Alex made one trip to Memphis, Tennessee, while Josephus made a trip up Red River. The boys could not be considered incorrigible and were pained because they had gone contrary to the advice of their parents, but they could not be stopped until they had earned enough to stop at Cheap John's in Cincinnati, and buy one of those cheap suits, and have a few pieces of coin to rattle in their pockets. When they returned home again they found the family packing up to move to Pomeroy. Father had been working there for some time and as the salt business was booming and he was making money at his trade, he concluded to make this his last move. We were perturbed when the news came that we were to pull away from our friends, from the boys and girls that we loved so well. It seemed to me that I would rather die than leave this town and people. We went to Mother and begged her to write Father and see if he would not reconsider, but as she would not interfere, we found that the die was cast and our doom was sealed. While we were in New Richmond our only sister was born, but lived only a few days.

When Father came home we had everything ready and soon were on our way to Pomeroy. For the children it was a sad leave, but as for Mother and Father they were anxious to go as they could not see any future for them or us in this town. We were standing on the wharf, the old St. James blew her long and doleful whistle, giving notice that she was soon to land and take on board this reluctant, downcast and dejected crowd. This is true so far as the children are concerned, but as for Father and Mother, they were elated. They knew that a tract of land had been purchased just at the edge of town which was to be our future home. They knew that stone masons were at that time working on the foundation upon which was soon to be erected a building large enough to accommodate this family which had increased to eight. We had been renting little houses here and there since we left Gallipolis, which does not accord with their ideas of real citizenship.

The St. James was the only packet on the river that carried a double cabin, that is, one for white passengers and one for colored. Between the lower deck and the upper cabin was a little segregated place for our people to eat and sleep. The beds were clean and the same food was served that was served in the cabin proper. This was the first and last time that the writer had ever been segregated. It was night when we left New Richmond and we stood back in a little recess in the rear of our Jim Crow cabin and sobbed and looked as long as we could see a light, then heartbroken and sleepy, we retired to our stateroom.

We landed at Pomeroy in October, 1869. We had heard of this town eight miles long and as far back as you could see, but did not understand the meaning. The town is a string town with one long street, the hills come out almost to the river, leaving just a narrow place for street. Many of the people live along the streams leading into the river. There is Karr's Run, Nailor's Run, Sugar Run, and Monkey Run. Many beautiful homes are built along these runs, the hills are lined with dwellings also.

We were favorably impressed at first sight, we had never seen such beautiful scenery as seemed to be everywhere apparent. On either side of that beautiful Ohio River towered hills almost to mountain heights and huge rocks overhanging the river as if to say, dare me and we will come tumbling down. From a dozen smoke stacks on either side of the river the smoke was curling upward which was evidence of the activities of the people of this section. The little tugs were chasing around making up tows for the larger boats while the big Pittsburgh steamers were rounding into the big bend with their acres of coal for southern consumption. Going through the street to our temporary home we found the street lined with wagons loaded with timber, hoop poles, staves, heading, waiting their turn to unload. Passing by the shops we could hear the men with adz and driver playing their tunes indicating that another barrel had been completed.

We were now satisfied that there were other places in the world besides Cincinnati, New Richmond, Southpoint and Gallipolis. We moved into a house belonging to Albert Hazlewood, a colored business and real estate man. This was a new house and suited our purpose very well until we could build our own house.

All were anxious to see the new layout and went on the hill next morning. We could hardly believe what our eyes beheld, a foundation that looked more like a foundation for a hospital or a hotel than a house. When we asked Father what he intended to build, he said that he intended to build a house large enough to give each one of his boys a room of his own, aside from living rooms, dining room, hall and kitchen. Another one of Father's large ideas. He overlooked the fact that as his boys grew to manhood one by one they would go out in the world to seek their own fortune, and that he and Mother would be lonesome in such a house. This is what happened.

Material for this house was produced at Hartford City, West Virginia four miles above Pomeroy, made into a raft and floated down to Enterprize landing. The contractor at once started the work of hauling the lumber and framing the building.

The schoolhouse is not the little red brick but a one-room frame structure with one very good he-man teacher. Our bunch started to school on the Monday morning following our arrival. We found here some very clever people, well advanced for their age and discovered that we would have to study to keep up with them. I had not at that time, nor have I at any time since, found children more eager for education. No town in the state of Ohio has produced and sent out into the world as many outstanding men and women as came out of this class. Joe Spears, a product of this little frame building, one of the leading orators of the Ohio and Kanawha valleys; James McHenry Jones, teacher, preacher, author, orator, and at the time of his death he was president of West Virginia Collegiate and Normal school, now the West Virginia State College; James E. Campbell, teacher, poet, orator, and one-time president of West Virginia Collegiate and Normal School; Fleming B. Jones, principal, Wheeling school, teacher, banker, first Negro in the United States of America to secure a charter for a National Bank; Calvin Morton, merchant; John L.

Jones, merchant; Ollie Wilson, teacher, orator; John R. Jefferson, teacher, principal of Parkersburg schools for 25 years, orator of no means but recognized ability; Edward Morton, teacher and scholar; Miss Bertha Morton and sister, teachers; Miss Irene Chilton Moats, teacher, principal and at this writing member of the advisory board, State of West Virginia; C. E. Jones, scholar, teacher, taught at West Virginia Collegiate Institute for 32 years; Harry Hazlewood, scholar, teacher, at this writing he is principal of the school at Huntington, West Virginia.

Time would fail me to cite more of the boys and girls who came out from under the rocks and hills of the first ward of Pomeroy. August 7th, 1870, Thomas Jefferson Jones was born. This was the 10th and last child born to Joseph and Temperance Jones. We moved into our new home, all were happy, Father and Mother extremely so. Father started by reading a chapter in the Bible and winding up with prayer. This was not unusual as we had family prayer from the beginning. I take pride in saying that my father was a man of prayer, even when we were thoughtless boys we loved to hear our father pray. Mother prayed, but Father always took the lead. His prayers were forceful, convincing, logical, he seemed to be talking to one who he knew to be a friend. I can say here and now that my father's prayers had more influence on my life than all the sermons that I have heard from a boy until the present. Their home life was beautiful, their Christian life was practical, in perfect harmony with their prayers. I never heard my parents use a vulgar word or a slang phrase. Father, at times, would flare up and whip a half-dozen of us, and when Mother said, "Stop," he would do so but never said a cross word to her. Those who read these lines may think me over-boasting in this picture, but language fails me to portray the lives of these almost divine characters.[12]

The only church in this part of town was the Wesleyan Methodist. My people, being Baptist, hesitated for some time before joining this church. For the sake of their growing family and finding, after all, they worshipped the same God that the Baptist worshipped, they joined and were followed by the two oldest boys, Alex and Josephus. After two or three years they concluded that they were out of their element and organized a Free Will Baptist church. Prof. T. J. Ferguson was installed as pastor. This church was in accord with their lifetime beliefs. They did not believe in what is called close communion, neither did they believe in pedo baptism. According to their interpretation of scripture, Christ was baptized in the Jordan and they could not live in a church that substituted sprinkling for baptism (immersion). The Free Will Baptists built a church home in Pomeroy and also in Middleport.

James H., at this time a bright and shining Christian boy and very forceful speaker, was ordained and given the oversight of these two churches.[13]

The organization of this church failed to create any ill feeling between these factions, they were not opposing factions, just two groups trying to carry out their idea of worship. At this time James H., or Jimmy as he was called, was the foremost scholar of the little frame building, had gone over the lower grade books until he knew them by heart and had passed the board and had taught one school. Father concluded that it was about time for the whites to open up central high school for our people.

Superintendent Flannigan was in school one Friday evening, Jimmy had read a paper just before he came in sight, giving the school authorities a good raking for not allowing him to go to high school. When the superintendent came in, Mr. Thomas Carr called Jimmy up and had him read the paper over again for Flannigan's benefit. When he had finished the paper, the superintendent came to him and congratulated him on his paper and told him to meet the school board Tuesday night and take the matter up with them, as he had his consent to enter high school. On Tuesday night Father and Jimmy met the board, Father brought up the matter and asked them to allow his son to make a statement. They gave him permission, and when he had finished his plea, the entire board gave their consent and sent him to Mr. Pace, the principal, who readily gave his consent by telling to go home and get his books and that he was glad to have him enter. This was the wedge that opened the Pomeroy High School to colored youths ten years before the Arnett bill was passed mixing the schools in Ohio. But for this move, the rest of the boys and girls from this little frame building would have been forced to wait ten years, when it would have been too late for most of them.[14]

Josephus, called Blossom, at 18 stood in his sock feet, six feet and three inches, weighed 198, a physical giant, said to be the strongest man in the Big Bend. He was as straight as an arrow and as pleasant as a basket of flowers. He was not only the pride of the family, but of the community as well. He took sick suddenly, the doctor was called and told them that he had quick galloping consumption, that his growth had been too rapid and that the trouble could not be arrested. This was a great shock to the family, though we continued to do everything that we could for him but to no avail. He sank slowly, but surely and passed away in his 20th year. Josephus knew that death was near, and calling his brothers to his bedside, left with them these words, "Study, study at school."

The following fall and winter Alex and I went back to the shop, the younger boys went back to school. The family was large and while it pained my parents to take me out of school, it was necessary. Father advised with me about it, I told him that I understood the situation, I knew his business and obligations and was willing to forgo my ambition for a while. I knew how they felt about it, I could see that it pierced their hearts to break the news to me, but when I agreed with them so readily they seemed greatly relieved. Alex is now his own man, he has been a good boy, hard worker, faithful and true to his parents, more cannot be expected of him. Since Josephus had passed away, I am the next in line and felt certain that by dint of economy Father and I could keep my four younger brothers in school and cancel his obligations.

Our place yielded abundantly this season, both in fruit and vegetables. We had corn to fatten four hogs, Mother made plum butter, apple butter, peach butter, and buried enough cabbage to last for the winter. We had wood on the place, cord wood for the fireplace and had ten tons of coal put in for the winter. The boys gathered walnuts and hickory nuts for our little home parties through the winter. We put four barrels of Russet and Roman Beauties in the cellar, besides we had canned fruit, tomatoes, beans and pickles of every description. Thus we were in a position to bid defiance to the hail, sleet and snow. Father and I made salt barrels for the German Salt Company in West Virginia, just opposite our home. We worked there because we were paid one cent more which meant from 20 to 25 cents more on the day. We crossed the river in a skiff, when the river was open. Sometimes the river would freeze over solid, in that case we would walk the ice.

Jimmy worked with me during vacation, he was not a cooper but an earnest worker and good gauger. We often led the shop, one week we made 101 barrels from the rough in 5 days, leading Morris and Henry Cousions by one barrel. This beat the record in this shop. In winter Father would not go to the shop. When the weather was severe, though, it was never too cold for us to go to singing school or to the debating society. Cold or hot, the people would turn out *en masse*. Most of the young people could read music. Father and Uncle Chas. Spears were always on hand and both were proficient teachers. Louis Carter developed into a very fine vocalist and could read music as fast as a chicken could pick up corn. All of our family could read music and all could sing, but Father was the best of all. Flem was a good tenor and Charley in later years became a good bass. Tommy, also, but if Alex, Jimmy and I ever won a prize for our good singing it would be because of the poor brand put up by the other fellows. Calvin Morton, Sr., James Black, Boliver Harris, J. M. Hazlewood, Joel Spears, Alex Jones, and others were the leaders in the debating society and were responsible for the credit brought to the community by the younger set.

The John Jay failure in 1873 brought on a panic in this country, it was sudden and caught the people unprepared. Poor people were fortunate if they could get a small sack of meal and a piece of meat. Mines, factories, shops and furnaces were closed, leaving labor without employment. As we have said before, Father never waits, when one job gives out he goes after another one. This time he goes into the medicine business. He had a recipe for the cure of ague and fever, and made up a large batch of this medicine, secured labels and went to Illinois where this disease was raging. He stayed there for several months, when he returned he had besides a good supply of money, a fine team consisting of two fine mules and a brand new wagon. We never knew why or how he got this team, nor what he did with it. We often teased Father and told him that we thought that he got the team when the owner was not looking. During this panic, William Ballard Harper and I took a contract with John J. Julah's Bromine Works, lifting bitter water salt, draining it and packing in barrels at so much a barrel. This proved to be a good thing for us as we made from three to five dollars a day. I turned this money over to my mother. I don't know how we would have fared during the absence of my father had it not been for this contract. All through this period I had change to spend and some to loan some of my unfortunate boy friends. I say unfortunate because they could not get any kind of work to do.

We were the only boys in town who had work, we would give our friends change to chip in for parties and go to socials. In those days they held religious revivals, real revivals without the aid of paid evangelists. At this time a revival started under the leadership of Rev. Donaldson, pastor of the Wesleyan Methodist Church. He was a good man and a convincing speaker. These people preached, prayed and sang for one week. When the meeting was well under way, they began inviting sinners to come not simply to give their hands to the preacher, but come and kneel at the mourner's bench, there to remain until their sins were forgiven. There were sixty-three young people who professed religion at this meeting, among whom were my friend Wm. Ballard Harner, James H. Jones and myself.

In 1875 my father had his affairs well in hand and was in position to send me back to school. The younger brothers had left me in the rear, but after three years of earnest work I completed the course in the little frame building. I was too old to enter high school so my teacher gave me lessons in the higher branches. To compensate him for his extra service I tried to teach him to sing, and read. He could not learn and seemed not to have the faintest idea of tone harmony or pitch, though well versed in the technique of music.

Having completed my course with Mr. Thomas Carr, I took the county examination and was employed to teach the little Rock-spring school situated on the outskirts of town. This school was called the stepping stone, as all of us stepped into this school and received our first experience in teaching. While I was teaching, James H. and Flem were in high school, they were the first of the colored boys to enter this school, in fact, the first colored boys in the state of Ohio to enter a white school. When I quit the shop I resolved never to cooper any more, I could not see any future for me at this fluctuating trade. I was past 21 and had been like my brother Alex, true to my parents, had not withheld anything from them. I had put in my life between Pomeroy and Cincinnati, had never been away from home a week in my life.

Our home was located on a hill overlooking the town, with a river view for miles above and below. One could stand in our hall door and see as far as Middleport, a distance of four or five miles. I had given much time and labor in beautifying this home, and it touched me to have to give it up. Then again, our home life was pleasant, the boys were chummy with each other, they went and came together and were happy in the company of each other. Mother and Father were moved to tears when I told them that I was going away. Father followed me to the train and wept bitterly. At this time there was much excitement in Perry County, on account of opening coal mines to colored miners and giving them some of the best positions in and around the mines. They rushed here by the hundreds from North, South, East and West to this new El Dorado. The company gave them every position that they could fill from miner to bookkeeper. This caused some ill feeling on the part of the white miners, as they feared that this induction of colored miners was for the purpose of pulling down wages, but the colored miners at the first opportunity joined the Knights of Labor and were among the first to join the U. M. of A., thus dispelling any fear of Negro miners coming to Perry County to pull down wages. As long as Negroes love to wear good clothes, set a good table, and educate their children, they will stand for a living wage if given a chance.

Alex Jones worked in the mine the winter of 1880-81 and was burned by the explosion of powder in his room. He returned home and spent the winter, in the spring he went back to the mine and entered into a contest for check-weighman and, after a hard battle, was elected. His work was so satisfactory that he was continued in this position as long as he remained in the valley.

I went to Rendville in 1881. My object was to secure the school and if possible get hold of enough money to complete my education. I was defeated in this as a young lady from Columbus had secured the school just a few days before my arrival. So there I was, all of the good positions taken, nothing left for me but mining or go back home. I determined to do neither, so I was offered a mule, but a mule never did appeal to me. Finally the superintendent told me not to leave, he would find something for me. In a few days he was in need of a dumper and offered that place to me. That work was too heavy for me, so in order to get me started he changed Ed Claxton from trimmer to dumper and gave me the position of trimmer.[15]

Soon after my installation in this job I organized a night school. Mr. Thomas Andrews, superintendent, allowed me to use the mine tipple as there was no other place available at this time. He had three boys and sent them and prevailed upon others to take advantage of this opportunity. With this addition, my salary was above the average.

In 1882, Jimmy graduated from the Pomeroy high school. He was the valedictorian of his class, being a natural born orator, he made a big hit in his address, capturing the entire town both white and black. His subject was "Iconoclast." Space will not permit me to give even some of the salient points in his address.

At this time the principal of the colored school of Wheeling, West Virginia, died, creating a vacancy there. Jimmy, J. J. Lee of Cambridge, Ohio, now of Columbus, Ohio, and one other man whose name I do not now recall, applied for the place. Mr. Lee withdrew his application on account of a contract with the Cambridge board of education, and threw his influence to Jimmy. His appearance and versatility, together with the good word from Mr. Lee, won him the appointment. After going to Wheeling he found it necessary to alter his name by prefixing "Mc," making it read J. McHenry Jones. There was another James H. Jones living in the city who had the pleasure of reading his mail and returning it to the office "opened by mistake." At this time he was corresponding with a young lady in Marietta, Miss Carrie Harrison, who afterward became his wife. To have this man reading those adoring passages was, to say the least, annoying, and to avoid any further mixup he made the above change.

The following year he was elected District Grand Master of the Odd Fellows Lodge of the state of Ohio. He became very popular in Odd Fellow circles throughout the nation. Being a forceful speaker and of such pleasing disposition he easily captured any audience. The Odd Fellows at this time were the strongest, richest and most powerful fraternal organization in the country among our people. To be a leader among them meant to be one of the leaders of the race. This was a worthy ambition that he had cherished from boyhood. At a meeting of the B.M.C., a fraternal delegate was to be elected to represent them at a meeting with the mother lodge in England. This was one of those opportunities that only comes once in a lifetime. McHenry and others of the leaders were put in nomination, he was elected and represented them in England the following year.[16]

In May, 1883, I gave up my job of trimmer at the coal mine. I had accomplished my purpose, had enlarged my wardrobe and had saved three hundred dollars. As I wanted to do something besides ordinary labor I left Rendville, and went to Springfield, and was employed by a Mr. Harvey who was a house painter and contractor. This gave me a chance to learn a trade. I learned rapidly and near the end of the season went to Kenton, Ohio, and bought a half interest in a business with one of the finest painters and decorators in the state. My object in going to Kenton, was to finish my trade and also to make it my future home. My health was poor in this town, the country was low and damp, I was sick, too sick to do anything but pay board, so Mr. Day bought back my interest and I started back to Pomeroy by way of Rendville, Ohio. I had been keeping company with Miss Sadie Broadis, the young lady who beat me getting the school. When I reached Rendville, she was with her father at McConnelsville, where he was holding a camp meeting. I drove there on Sunday morning, a distance of 23 miles, and spent the day with her, returning in the evening. McHenry was the principal attraction at this meeting. The officers of the largest and richest church in McConnelsville (white) asked him to take charge of their church, they made the salary attractive, but he refused to accept as he was tied up with the Wheeling school.

When I returned to Rendville, I found that Mr. Jas. Johnson, the man with whom I had boarded for two years, had started a grocery store depending on a son of about 14 years of age to run the business. Finding that he had not the least idea of business, he asked me to take an equal partnership in the business. The proposition suited me as I had nothing to do except go home and sit down until spring. We invoiced his stock and I matched it with cash and began my career.

We had no commercial rating, which made it necessary for me to go to Columbus each month to buy goods. In that way I had a chance to get acquainted with business men and ways. Competition was sharp and I soon found that to compete, it was necessary to have a larger turnover. I ran this little business for about one year, turning over about $250.00 a month. This did not keep me busy, so I took a course in business by correspondence and a course in reading. I did not go out to anything, just attended to business and books.

Over one half of the people of this town were Negroes and most of the business was in the hands of the white race. Rev. Hammond, Dr. I. S. Tuppins and I assembled some of our most progressive citizens and organized a Miner's cooperative store with capital limited to $10,000. Thomas Preston was elected president; Dr. I. S. Tuppins, secretary; Floyd Tyler, treasurer; J. L. Jones, manager, with a full set of directors. Shares were sold at $25.00 each. Forty paid in full at our first meeting, giving us a working capital of $1,000 to start with. We absorbed the Johnson and Jones store, using the same building. In 1884 one thousand dollars would buy more goods than two thousand dollars would buy today. This money was placed at my disposal. I bought $800.00 worth of goods, leaving $200.00 for replacement.

We sold for cash to all except members of the company, which was our first and greatest mistake. I urged upon the directors to amend the by-laws to read: "No member can deal out in any month over 80% of the amount of his investment." As several of them kept boarders they turned down the proposition. Some would use as much as $70.00 a month and leave a balance on payday.I was anxious to succeed and kept up a howl on this sort of business, but as the large families were in the majority, they would out vote us on all such propositions. Our volume was large, our overhead was small and in spite of our directors I managed to show a gain of 25% for the first year.

In this year, 1884, the writer was married to Miss Sarah D. Broadis. Miss Broadis was born in Virginia, and came to this state with her parents when a small child. After graduating from the Columbus high school, she came to Rendville, and taught three years in the public school. We have had an army of colored teachers since then, including one of her daughters, but she was the first colored person to teach school in Perry County, and the first of any race to teach in Rendville, Ohio.

Flem and Charley finished high school and began teaching the following year. Flem made the four-year course in three years. He was given the room in Rendville, made vacant by the resignation of Miss Broadis. Charley began his career as teacher in Gallia County, Ohio. These three boys loved their chosen profession and kept abreast of their work by spending time in Summer School at the University of Michigan, Oberlin College and the Case School of Applied Science, Cleveland, Ohio.

Flem taught one year at Rendville, the following year was elected to the principalship of the Middleport School. The room made vacant by him at Rendville, was filled by the election of Charley.

Thomas finished his grade work and enters high school as the two other boys are leaving. Father and Mother are happy now and will have accomplished their ambition with the graduation of their youngest son. This is the end over which they had bent their lives if something unforeseen should happen to them, the brothers will see him through. All five of the boys are drawing good money and are chipping in with regularity to keep the home fires burning, this is all extremely gratifying to know that they can relax after years of ceaseless toil.

At Middleport, Flem got into a heated newspaper controversy with the Meigs County teachers, the question was asked, "Why do we invert the divisor in division of fractions?" The teachers all contend that it is done for convenience while he takes an opposite view and proves his contention to the satisfaction of all.

Again he wrote Mr. Harvey, calling his attention to errors in his grammar, this called for an exchange of many letters between them. Finally Mr. Harvey capitulated and promised to make the correction in his revised edition.

In the year 1885 Zenobia Broadis Jones, daughter of J. L. and Sarah D. Jones, was born. This is the first child born to this generation, in fact, none of the boys except the writer have taken the responsibility of a family. All are proud of their little niece, and one by one they find excuse to come to Rendville to see her.

After three years in business in some form, we have concluded to make it our life work. I like to buy and sell, also the daily contact with people. I like it because I have found that there is no color in business. From boyhood I could not understand why we as a race had to buy all the boots and shoes, all the flour and meat and such and the other fellow get all the profit. I knew, also that the Cooperative store though prosperous would in time be a thing of the past, so a business place about two doors north of our store was for sale. I bought it, repaired the upper story and moved my family in and thus cut the rent, let the storeroom to a merchant until such time as I would need it, that time was not long coming. In 1887 a slump came in the coal business, when most of our company went west and the directors proposed to turn over the store to me, the proposition was accepted. I took over their stock assumed their responsibilities and moved into my own building. In buying this building and with the expense incident to the transfer of the business I found myself short on cash and borrowed

$300.00, to freshen up my stock and rushed into the business world under the firm name of J. L. Jones.[17]

In 1888 McHenry was married to Miss Carrier Harrison of Marietta, Ohio. Their life was ideal for the duration of five years. At the table one morning she took suddenly ill and died before the doctor could reach her.

After the death of his wife he became very restless, he was constantly on the go during the period of vacation. Often called to assist someone in religious meetings, or to deliver a lecture or series of lectures, or attend a Grand or District meeting of some of the many fraternal orders with which he was affiliated. He was in great demand as a political speaker, often called to speak in Ohio and Pennsylvania, as well as in his adopted state. He also appeared before many audiences as lecturer. Here are some of his subjects: "Is the Good Time Coming?"; "Frederick Douglass;" "don't;" "The Triple Tie;" "Abraham Lincoln;" and others. In 1897 he married Miss Elizabeth Moore of Cincinnati, Ohio. At this time Miss Moore was teaching with him in the Wheeling school.

In this year he represented the United Order of Odd Fellows in England, being the first to bear the greetings of his order to the mother lodge or A.M.C. at Bolton, England, Whit-week.

In England he was treated more as a prince than a common citizen. He was given 21 banquets, three by members of Parliament, he spoke at them all, not because he wanted to but because they insisted upon him at every occasion.

McHenry happened to be in England at the time of the Queen's Jubilee and with some of his English friends rode in the procession. He wore a Prince Albert suit and silk plug hat together with his tanned complexion gave him the appearance of a foreigner. The people along the line of march mistook him for an Indian prince and ran after his carriage cheering the prince. He always acknowledged by doffing his hat. This was kept up through the entire line. After finishing his mission in England, he visited Scotland, Wales and the Continent. Upon return home he published his trip in the Odd Fellows' Journal. Before leaving for England he had been elected to the presidency of the school at Institute, West Virginia. His friends, including Governor Atkinson insisted upon his giving up the school at Wheeling and launching out into broader fields, but he loved the people at Wheeling and they loved him. Both white and colored prevailed upon him to stay but, partly because of the insistence of his friend the governor and the chance to make a place for his brother, he accepted the position.[18]

Flem left Middleport and at that time was teaching in Chillicothe, Ohio, having been elected as principal sometime before.

The school at Chillicothe was a larger and better school than Middleport, and Flem was well satisfied with it. However, when McHenry went to Institute, Flem filed application and was elected to the school made vacant by his resignation. The people of Wheeling did not receive Flem with open arms, as they seemed to think that no one could manage the school like McHenry. While the two brothers were different as to type, they soon found that Flem was a master of the school room. Flem was not active in the affairs of the city, he only made occasional speeches, but never political. As I write I think that he was unsurpassed.

Charley continued with the school at Rendville, Ohio. While there he was married to Miss Mary F. Vance. Miss Vance moved to Rendville with her parents when a child, attended he public school of this place until she finished the course and was one of the first to graduate in the mixed school. Mary was loved by the people of this place because of her lovely disposition and activities in church and Sunday school work.

My mother was pleased with Charles's selection as she was acquainted with Mr. and Mrs. Vance and knew that he made choice from a good Christian family. The two boys were to have a double wedding but for some reason, Flem did not marry for some weeks after. Flem married a young lady, Miss Mayme Morris, a teacher in the Middleport school. Miss Morris was born in Middleport and educated in the public school of that city. She taught with him in Middleport and Chillicothe, but dropped out after leaving Chillicothe.

Charley Jones was considered one of the best teachers that ever taught in this county. It seems that his old scholars never tire of talking about him and the last time he visited us they swarmed around him, each trying to get in a word about the old days.

President Parks, president of the schools of the district, came to Charlie and asked him if he would give up his school for a while and go to Hatfield and take charge of the school there. The Hatfield scholars had run all the teachers away, and they had no one who could control the school. Charlie told him that he would go if they would make it interesting. They asked him what advance he would ask, he told them and the deal was made. This was a purely white community, not a colored person living in the town. Securing a boarding house he started his school the following Monday morning. The people and scholars treated him nicely. The first week the school increased from three to fifty-three and the interest continued as long as he remained with them. In some way his reputation reached West Virginia as he received a message from the board of regents to report at Institute at once. He resigned at once and took train for Institute, where he was employed as a teacher in that Institution.

Thomas finished his course in high school. He could have gone into the same profession, but refused to seek employment in the school room as he contended that the family had quite enough teachers and that he would seek other employment. He went to Wyoming, with a lot of men with the promise of work in a store. Failing in this he came back as far as Ft. Scott, Kansas, from there to Arkansas, working there a few months returned back to Pomeroy. Finally, growing tired and restless at home without anything to do, wrote me that he would leave home within a few days for Chicago. I wired him to stay at home until he heard from me. I wrote my brother-in-law, Mr. W. B. Wright at Cleveland, Ohio, who was secretary to the president of the Nickel Plate Railroad, recommending Thomas and urging upon him to find something for him to do. Mr. Wright secured him a position as assistant baggage master with the Nickel Plate Railroad. After working there for several years he thought he had enough money to go to college and matriculated at the Western Reserve as a dental student. Completing the course he at once opened an office in the city of Cleveland, Ohio.

Alex resigned his position with the miners and went west, locating at Fort Scott, Kansas. He married while living there, two children were born to them, Wert and a girl who died in infancy. This death was followed by the death of the mother. Shortly thereafter, Alex returned home, bringing his son with him. That year he joined the Baptist Association, was ordained an Elder and was called to the pastorate of the home church. After one year he was called to the Baptist church of Parkersburg, West Virginia. Serving there two years, resigned and came back home. While at home our house caught fire, the fire caused by a defective flue, being high on the hill and no fire apparatus the building soon burned to the ground.

Father and Mother came at once to Rendville, and lived with us until another home could be provided for them. A very desirable home was purchased on the street where they were surrounded by the best people of the town, white and colored. The fire seemed Providential. Since the boys are seldom at home and for them to be on the hill alone in that big house has been annoying to us and now that they were on the street near their church everything went well for a while.

The following winter both were stricken with pneumonia, Alex and I were with them during this siege, they finally recovered but were never the same, seemed weak and unable to regain their strength. McHenry came down from Institute and moved them into the house with him. They had a nice home with everything that heart could wish, the faculty and student body made much over them, everybody was kind and even affectionate, Charley and his children came in every few hours to laugh and joke with them, Mother always seemed happy under any conditions, but Father never could feel at home only under his own roof. In fact he felt that his work was done, he had lived to see his boys grown and doing well, and that was the single purpose of his life. He contended that his work was done and he wanted to go home to rest. Senility or the infirmity of old age had set in, he refused to talk, his appetite was entirely gone. Ready, willing and anxious to go, he did not die, he went to sleep December 13, 1904. He that liveth and believeth in me shall never die. Believeth thou this? St. John, 11th chapter and 26th verse. His body was removed to Pomeroy, and interred in the family lot, Beechwood cemetery. Ben Biggs, the old undertaker when telling us goodbye, said, "Boys, you have put away one of the best citizens of Pomeroy and honest to the core, he has stood for the funeral expenses of more poor people than any one in town and does not owe me one cent. John McQuig, the cashier of the First National Bank, would loan my father any amount of money that he would ask for without any kind of security, his word was sufficient.

After my father died, I never saw my mother again in life. I wrote her on the 13th of July, 1905, my birthday, and sent her under separate cover some nice presents. I told her that instead of receiving that I prefer giving and all that I charged her was to tell me how old I am today, when I was with her I knew my age but since I left her I have told so many different stories about my age that I have really forgotten it. When McHenry read the letter to her she laughed heartily and took the parcel to show it to Joseph, but came back and said to them, Joseph is not there. This was about six in the evening, she retired in a short time and took suddenly ill early next morning and passed away about 12 hours after receiving my letter. Her body was brought to Pomeroy and interred beside her husband. This grand old pair never had anything showered upon them but love. Their sons in both cases acted as pallbearers and lowered them to their last resting place.

Dr. Thomas continued his practice in Cleveland, with varied success for abut five years. While there he became engaged to a young lady and as money was not coming in as fast as he thought it should, he felt the call to go south where he would have a larger constituency. His choice of the southern cities was Mobile, AL, where he went and at once equipped a nice dental parlor. His first move after he had set up was to call on the white dentists of the city, they told him as with one voice, that they were glad to have him in the city as they did not want the Negro trade. He dived into the business and his income was away beyond his fondest dream. He was not well when he left Cleveland, though he did not advise us. A lady called me from Cleveland and asked me if I knew that Dr. Tom was sick? I wired Mr. Wright who had friends in Mobile, and who could dead-head a message for me. He wired at once to his friend who on investigation found that it was true. He had been sick for months and was unable to walk to and from his office. I got busy and found out the trouble from him. I at once notified his brothers at Institute and Wheeling. We decided to send him to a higher altitude and in a few weeks he was off for San Antonio, Texas. To keep down his expenses, also to keep down worry on his part, I had the boys to send me a check for a stipulated amount each month, then I would register the cash to him and thus save him the trouble of hunting someone to identify him.

He had the best medical attention that could be procured and the first few months gained forty pounds. This greatly encouraged him. His hope did not last long as he began to lose weight until he lost the forty pounds gained the first four months. Then he wrote my daughter, Zenobia, stating that he had about given up the struggle and wanted to come home. I wired the money and he came at once to Rendville. This poor boy had spent hundreds of dollars with specialists and doctors in the vain attempt to recover his health and at the same time keep back his real condition from his family. After he reached home and rested up for a few days, I took him to Columbus to a specialist and had a thorough examination, when he had finished he shook his head and refused to make a statement. As we left the office Thomas said, "I will not allow you boys to spend another dollar on me." I told him that we intended to stay with him until the last dollar was spent and then we would mortgage our homes and think nothing of it if by so doing he could stay the ravages of his trouble.

At home my wife treated him as if he were her own brother and the children were as attentive as if he were a child, and oh, how he did appreciate it. We had the best doctor that we could secure against his protest for he knew it was futile. At Cleveland he roomed with a young doctor who had a tubercular throat, and he traced his trouble to this contact. He went to Institute to see Father and Mother also McHenry, Charley and family, and while there his voice came back but only for a short time. Charley shouted when he heard his voice ring out in a clear tone but it was only that they might hear his voice for the last time. . . . He returned home and grew steadily worse and knowing that his time was short he asked me to send for Flem as he had never seen his boys. I sent for them and notified the other boys of his condition. Flem and family came at once, Charley also. McHenry was not at home at the time.

As a scholar he was the most thorough of the family, always a quiet seeker after knowledge. McHenry as well as Flem and Charley make this concession. While in Cleveland he lived in the public library. His mind was always fixed on preparation for the future activities of life. He had no fear of death, but often said to me that he would love to live just two more years to show to the world that he was not a failure. This privilege was not granted. He was sitting on the side of the bed talking to me, and unattended, lay down, closed his eyes as if going to sleep. Resting on my arm he breathed his life out October 15th, 1905. His body was removed to Pomeroy and interred in the family lot.

After McHenry returned from England, he entered immediately into the work as president at Institute. He proved himself to be a good executive, the school began to grow, large appropriations were made, new buildings were erected, the faculty was enlarged, students began to pour in from West Virginia, Ohio, and other states. This phenomenal growth continued until today West Virginia Collegiate Institute is one of the outstanding schools of its class in this country.

McHenry made an addition to American Literature by the publication of *Hearts of Gold*, which was widely distributed and eagerly ready by all classes. I heard Judge Morris Donahue of the Federal Court make during a speech, three quotations from *Hearts of Gold*. This one, I remember: "When the Englishman goes back to the Thames, when the Frenchman goes back to the Seine, when the German goes back to the Rhine, then the Negro may go back to the Congo." This was written during a period of controversy over sending a Negro back to Africa. He wrote a novel, *A Strange Transformation*. It was in the hands of the publisher when he failed, and the manuscript was misplaced. His last contribution was *The Bluevaynes* which was ready for publication at the time of his death. His purpose was to give up school work, build a home in Wheeling, West Virginia, and write for the rest of his time.

The last address made by McHenry was at Seattle, Washington. He represented the Methodist Episcopal Church (white) of West Virginia, at a meeting of the International Epworth League, embracing the Methodist Churches of the North, South and Canada. On account of his speech there the Honorable H. C. McWhorter of West Virginia makes the following tribute:

On our recent trip to the West at Seattle we took in the International Epworth League of the Methodist Church, South, and the Methodist Episcopal Church of Canada. On the third day of the convention, addresses were made by speakers from all the churches represented, on the topic "The Epworth League and the enthronement of Christ," Professor J. McHenry Jones of Charleston being one of the speakers. This was Professor Jones's last appearance before a public audience; the hall was crowded to its utmost capacity. It was getting late, and the people wearied, he held that vast audience of 6,000 or 8,000 in undivided attention to the close of his magnificent address, which was thought by many to be the best and most eloquent made on that occasion. I heard very many expressions to that effect. We were made to feel proud of West Virginia. As Professor Jones has just passed away, I think it due to his memory to say this of the last speech of his life.

H. P. McWHORTER

From Seattle, he went down the coast of California, stopping at Pasadena to pay a visit to the family of Professor W. A. Payne, after a few days visit he started back East.

His first stop was Cincinnati, Ohio. The District Lodge of Odd Fellows was in session. He made a short talk to them, gave them a gold Odd Fellows collar given to him by the Grand Lodge of England. He told them that he would never see them again; gave them his benediction and started for his home at Institute. McHenry was sick when he left my house going West, sick when he reached Seattle, sick when he reached Cincinnati, and worse when he reached home. My wife and I spent ten days with him after he returned from the West. He kept on his feet but it was evident that he was growing worse. The last Sunday that we ever spent together was in the yard in front of his house, and being in a reminiscent mood he made this remark, "I have never done anything in my life that I would be ashamed for my mother to know." Knowing him as I did from youth up I could accept this statement without question. Some weeks after we came home I was in Columbus, Ohio, attending the Baptist National Convention. I met a lady from West Virginia who asked if I knew that McHenry was worse, and as I had not, I rushed home and my daughter, Ethel and I took the first train out for Institute. My brother, Alex was there also. He did not recognize us until the next day. Looking up and recognizing Ethel he said, "I know, I know." I asked him, "What do you know, Jimmy?" He said, "I am going to die." Then I asked him, "Are you afraid to die?" To which he replied, "No, I am not, for God always takes care of His people." If ever I had any fear or doubt it was removed after that statement. Then he called for his wife, Elizabeth, but his words were incoherent, and in another minute, he passed away.

This was on September 22nd, 1909. He was advertised to make an Emancipation Day speech in Pittsburgh on that day.

The funeral oration was delivered by Dr. I. V. Bryant, pastor of the First Baptist Church of Huntington, West Virginia. I must quote one paragraph from that wonderful oration. "As to Christian character, it would be difficult for me to name a man of more unquestionable piety. I have known him from childhood to manhood. Even when a small youth he showed unmistakable signs of genuine piety. Even before he was old enough to attend public schools he showed indication of a burning thirst for knowledge. At the school he stood at the head of his class in every branch of study. While even a boy he exhibited characteristics uncommon to childhood. He sought the company of men instead of boys. Professors of school, ministers of the gospel and men of matured minds were his companions. While yet a boy in tender years he was ordained to preach the gospel and held great audiences spellbound. I have carefully watched his career and have been in close touch with him all during these years. His whole life has been one of an upward march."[19]

Following was a tribute of reverence by W. L. Hueston, Grand Master of the Grand United Order of Odd Fellows, followed by Governor Wm. E. Glasscock and ex-governor Geo. W. Atkinson. His body was interred in a beautiful lot purchased especially for that purpose, along the main walkway leading from the station to the school. By order of the State Board of Regents a memorial tablet was erected and suitably worded in the walls of the main building of the West Virginia Colored Institute.

The following summer with appropriate ceremony this tablet was dedicated, memorial address was made by ex-Senator Sherman Durst, a lifetime friend of McHenry's. Biography was read by Miss Charlotte Campbell, music by the school double quartette, Mrs. Charles Mitchell presiding at the piano. Unveiled by Miss Eunice Jones, daughter of Professor C. E. Jones.

The new administration building at Institute, erected since the death of McHenry Jones, has chiseled in the arch over the door at the main entrance an everlasting monument to his memory.

Professor C. E. Jones was the first of the Jones boys to go to Institute as a teacher. At that time James Monroe Hazlewood was a member of the board of regents, he and the Jones boys were reared in the same Ohio town, and were always close friends. Mr. Hazlewood wired C. E. to report at Institute at once at which time he was employed. This was before the coming of McHenry. The teachers associated with them were Profs. Byrd Prillerman, Colonel J. M. Canty, E. M. Burgess, Mr. Spriggs, Mary E. Eubanks, A. W. Curtis. There may have been others but these I recall. When Charlie would visit us or when I would have occasion to go there he always spoke of these associates in the very highest terms.

After they were properly installed a little trouble arose. His satanic majesty, always busy, started the rumor that C. E. was not competent to teach chemistry. This same fellow started trouble in heaven before the world was created. He caused heaven to shake and as Milton puts it, "Had Earth been then she too had to her center shook." It was only a matter of jealousy on the part of one in no way connected with the school. Charley never held any bad feelings toward the person who started this rumor, he knew as we all know that jealousy is inborn and can only be disposed of by prayer and fasting. Since few people pray and none fast we are all more or less tarred with this stick. This person continued to busy himself until it reached the ears of the Board of Regents through a charge made to them. Charley was called before them for examination. The complainant, McHenry, J. M. Hazlewood and others were present. The board went on with their examination until they were convinced that he was perfectly competent, then turned around and asked, "Who said this man did not know chemistry?" The gentleman who filed the charge was present but could only drop his head and slink away. Charley was not only competent to teach chemistry, but could and did teach every subject taught in the normal department of school.

At the time of his death he was the oldest teacher at Institute, in point of service, and during these years every student had some subject under him. Every Institute boy and girl finished at this school will remember him because of the interest he took in them. He was personally interested in them. He did not teach for bread and butter alone, but the trend of his great life was to build up and render service. I have sat on his porch during commencement season and noticed young men who had finished their course present him with many tokens of love and appreciated, which would so touch his heart that he could not restrain tears.

After he had spent a few years at Institute he decided to make it his permanent home, and bought a lot from Mr. Scott Brown consisting of one-half acre. This lot was not for sale but he had so ingratiated himself into the good graces of Mr. Brown that he finally consented to sell him the lot. On this lot was erected a very nice two-story residence in which he spent his days.

He could not have chosen a better place to rear his family, under the shadow of one of our best schools, where the moral and religious influence was and is the very best obtainable. His one ambition was to rear his family in this splendid environment and instill in them the principles of Christianity. He as well as his wife, Mary, became Christians in an early day, and like his father instituted family prayer in the home. He was a lover of the Bible and imbibed its principles in everyday life. He was not of the more-holy-than-thou type but rather of the clean and practical, who could enjoy a good joke or clean story, especially when told by Sherman Guss, Scott Brown or Mr. Elijah Hurt. He was a public school teacher but could not be called a public man as he did not care for publicity. To enjoy his growing, interesting family, his books, his church and Sunday school and his local friends seemed to make up the sum total of his pleasure.

There were eight children in this family, three were born in Rendville, Ohio, and five in Institute. West Virginia.

James McHenry, the oldest, finished at Institute, and taught for several years. When the call came for soldiers to go to the front in order to make this a better country in which to live, James was one among the first to go. Returning from the war he at once set out in his pursuit of higher knowledge. He took up dentistry in Meharry Medical College, Nashville, Tennessee. Finishing, he at once opened a dental parlor in the city of Chicago, Illinois. As this city was filled to overflowing with young Negro professional men struggling for an existence, James concluded to go to some field where the competition would not be so keen, so he moved to Alton, Illinois. His business was very satisfactory.

Bulah, the second child died at a very early age.

Eunice had just finished her course in school and was almost suddenly cut off by death. This was the first real shock for this family in which we were all equally pained. Eunice was one of those young ladies that won the heart of everyone who knew her. She was beautiful, modest, attractive and brilliant. She was very talented in music, having climbed to the tenth grade in piano lessons. A very bright future in this field of endeavor was without a doubt in store for her. It was said by many who heard her play the piano that she had no equal in touch and interpretation of classical selections. But the hopes of her relatives and friends that she would some day be a noted pianist were soon cut off. She died at the youthful age of sixteen years.

Charles Connelly, the next in line, after finishing his normal course went to Ohio University at Athens, Ohio, remaining there until the war was over at which time he went with his brother James McHenry to Meharry Medical College, remaining there until he finished his course in dentistry. He came back to Chicago, Illinois, and found employment in the Post Office. He did not remain in the Post Office long until he opened his dental parlors. Few, if any, of the young dentists in Chicago, are going faster than Connelly, according to our informant.

Margaret and Eula received their college degrees the next day after the interment of their father. After the commencement was over Professor Davis came to the platform to make his final announcements, among which was the appointment of Margaret Jones assistant music teacher of the school. This was a great surprise to everyone and so pleasing that an uproarious spontaneous applause went up and lasted for several minutes. Through it all Miss Margaret did not show the least sign of emotion.

Eulah Fay had been assigned to a good school in another part of the state. She was well prepared and would make her way. She became a Christian in early youth, she drank deeply of the teaching received around the hearthstone.

Maurice Reid, finished school in 1928 and immediately secured a position as secretary to Capt. G. E. Ferguson. Capt. Ferguson, an influential business man, particularly in real estate, a great power in politics, with push and stability, clean living and square in dealing with his fellow-men, was appointed to the directorship of the State Bureau of Negro Welfare & Statistics, by Governor Wm. G. Conley, July 1, 1929, due to these qualifications above mentioned. No doubt others applied for the position for secretary to the director in this department of the state government and it was later brought to my attention that fifty other applications were filed for this position secured by Maurice. This is one of the most promising young men of the race, he has in him all the elements of success. He is the very type of his father, not over versatile, but as deep as still water. He started out in this world with an unimpeachable character, this is evidenced by his first appointment. Besides fitness, the next requisite is character. Maurice has both, hence his appointment. Maurice became a member of Kappa Alpha Psi fraternity in 1927.

Edward Francis and Louis Earl are yet in school. At last account they were getting along nicely. They are both studious and we are all hopeful as to their ultimate outcome.

It is not our purpose to say over much about these young people, they are just beginning, they are in the making. I as the oldest member of this family now living feel certain that you will carry out the purpose of your progenitors, that you will live up to our expectations. Father and Mother prayed and sacrificed, threw luxuries to the wind that you might have advantages. While we cannot say much about you in this early stage of your existence, we trust that future biographers may be able to lift you up so high that the generation to which your parents belonged would, if living, have to tiptoe to touch the bottoms of your feet.

C. E. Jones was a home man. He made few trips for pleasure. His wife often urged upon him to take a vacation, but he felt that he could better spare the money to meet some of his more pressing obligations. He knew that his income was small, he knew also that his task was a stupendous one and to make his income cover these obligations required the most rigid economy. To visit in the summer season meant to neglect his garden, which he was passionately, yes religiously, fond of. When we last visited him in this season of the year, the first thing that he would point out would be his garden. We noticed that even the poles with which he stuck his peas and beans were uniform, the rows were straight, the hills were rounded up as if they were moulded in the same mould. Everything in that garden showed a perfect mind and one in love with his work. If there was ever a man who could make two blades of grass grow where one formerly grew, that man was C. E. Jones.

Charlie and I had a few trips together, in 1893. We were together at the World's Fair. I went one day ahead of him. He went by way of Cleveland. Dr. Tom joined him there, we met in Chicago, and boarded at the same place during our stay. Charlie and I always enjoyed the pleasure of being together and often for no reason other than to socialize for a few hours. These meetings were usually at Gallipolis or Pomeroy. Five years ago I wrote him to meet me in Athens, Ohio, on a certain date and we would go to Cincinnati, and spend a week together. He answered by return mail saying, that the proposition just suited him, and that he would be there on the date named. We met and took the B&0 for Cincinnati. We had many friends and acquaintances in the city but preferred not to meet any of them as we were out for the sole purpose of being alone and to go as we pleased without any formality; we wanted to keep going without interference, we did not want to go to some house and take a meal then sit and talk for the rest of the day. We had the hack man take us to the best hotel in the city that would accommodate us. I have forgotten the name of the hotel but it was well up to his recommendation. The second day we were going downtown and met a lady friend who seemed dazed to meet us on the streets of the city. She asked us when we came in and why we did not call her up and many such questions. We told her that we did not intend to leave the city without calling on her. This did not suit her as she insisted upon us going to the hotel and bringing our baggage to her house and remaining there as long as we were in Cincinnati.

It had been 55 years since we left New Richmond, and while we were quite small we remembered a little play girl by the name of Jennie Boone, so we spent a part of two days visiting there. We first went to the house of a Mrs. Moore who was the sister of Jennie Boone Simpson. Jennie lived about two miles in the country, her sister called her up and told her that she would be out to her house in a short time bringing two old friends.

About 6 o'clock that evening Mrs. Moore and her son drove us together with another sister by name Fannie Wilkins to the home of Jennie Boone Simpson. We spent the better part of the night there talking and singing. Charlie seemed more than pleased at the splendid reception received from these people. The Simpsons and the Boones are fine well-to-do people, and just as nice as can be found anywhere. When the people found out who we were and that we had lived there before most of them were born, they seemed to vie with each other as to who could do the most in the way of entertaining us. When we left the city for Cincinnati; the people crowded around the bus as if we were people of note, having loaded us with cigars and fruit of all kind. Charlie was always a man of tender heart and so on account of this manifestation of love of the real sort it brought tears to his eyes. Our last morning in Cincinnati was spent with Mrs. Richard Connelly, taking in some of the places of interest, in the afternoon we went with Mr. Connelly to the baseball park. Charlie was a Reds rooter and had the pleasure of seeing them win from the Wolverines.

We left Cincinnati the next morning for Athens, where we parted, he going to Nelsonville, Ohio, to visit Dave Wayne, his wife's uncle. This was the last and most pleasant trip that we ever had together.

Shortly after going to his work the next year I had a letter from Mary stating that Charlie had taken suddenly ill and urging me to come to Institute at once. I reached there the next evening and found him slightly better. He continued to improve and within a week he was able to resume his duties. It was thought by many it was due to over-exertion and worry, indeed this thought was shared by some of his family, but ten years before this a doctor's examination disclosed the fact that his trouble was due to the heart and that his heart was out of line. I have learned that the local physician at Institute found this to be true.

The next meeting was a sad one. It was on the occasion of the death of my son, John L. Jr. It had not been but a few months since he paid a visit to his uncle, the first time they had met for many years. While Charlie was here he went to Columbus to meet Zenobia, who was rushing home from California, they had not met for about 20 years also. It was the common remark by all of his friends that he looked better than for years. He remained with us for about one week before returning turning home. Zenobia, Ethel, Earl and I followed him to the station and gave him up with reluctance. This was the last time that any of us ever looked upon him. God was kind to us on this morning of January 29th, 1927, and veiled our eyes that we might not see that this dear brother and uncle was the next of the family to be called to his reward. On August 6th, 1928, we had a message stating that Charlie had passed away. Funeral service was held in the school chapel. Sermon was preached by Dr. I. V. Bryant, D.D., of Huntington, West Virginia. Interment was made beside his brother, McHenry, at Institute, West Virginia.

If there is anything that I can do to alleviate the condition of mankind, to make his future brighter, and better, let me do it now while I am passing, as it is certain that I shall never pass this way again.

Sixteen months after Charlie died Mary, his wife passed away. She made a great effort to conceal her feelings from her children. Her suffering was silent and intense, her smile and facial appearance were the same, but was not an index of her feeling. These two lives were so intertwined that one would not live without the other. Mary made a good fight though a losing one. She sent us word late Sunday evening by messenger that as soon as she got a little better she intended to pay us a visit. Before the message reached us the fatal telegram came. Some months before I sent her a book by Dr. Lyman Abbott, *The Other Room*. She read it with great interest and was so pleased with it that she had some of her friends read it also. She liked one passage which says, "Death is Not a Cessation but a Continuation." This being true, they are still intertwined, and together. They are developing into that higher life and will march together on coronation day and help to crown Him Lord of all.

James McHenry Jones, Charles Edward Jones, Mary F. Jones, and two children, Bulah Jones and Miss Eunice Jones, were buried in the same enclosure at Institute, West Virginia.

Thirty years ago Fleming Bertram Jones, following the advice of his physician, left Wheeling for Oklahoma. He with his family consisting of wife and two boys came to Rendville to pay us a short visit and to meet McHenry and Charlie before going. He had been advised that the climate along the Ohio Valley was too severe and that it was move or die. To go from one place to another is not bad if it is of your own choosing, but to be forced against your will is, to say the least, sad indeed. I went to the station with Mayme and the boys while Flem went ahead to purchase their tickets. I told Mayme that it pained me to see them leaving for that far away country, to which she replied, "Sannie, we can make it. I can cook, wash, and iron, I can teach school and teach music. If Flem can take care of the boys I am sure that I can do the rest." My apprehension was dispelled after this showing of such dogged confidence and determination. Their first stop was at Martlesville, they lived there ten months, was sick most of the time. Went to Boley September 1st, 1909. Was elected to the faculty of the Creek and Seminole University in the capacity of dean, or acting president. Mrs. Jones was Director of Music. He entered the Farmers and Merchants Bank as bookkeeper in the year of 1910, and was made assistant cashier in 1911 and held this position until 1921 at which time he resigned to assist in the organization and establishment of the First National Bank of Boley, Oklahoma.

The First National Bank of Boley opened its doors for business September 10th, 1921. I want to emphasize the fact that Fleming Bertram Jones was the first cashier of a national bank in the United States owned and operated by Negroes. The Douglass National Bank, of Chicago did not receive its charter until June 1922, just 10 months after the Boley Bank. In 1914 they built a home in Boley, later they bought a farm exactly one mile east of town on the main highway between Oklahoma and Fort Smith. Mrs. Mayme Jones taught music in the Oklahoma Normal and Industrial Institute for eight years. Since that she has confined herself to private teaching—having a class never less than 40, from that to 55, in fact she is acknowledged to be the outstanding music teacher in Eastern Oklahoma. The weight and impress of the Jones hand has been and is seen in the music life of Boley since they first went to that town, both in instrumental and choral. Bishop Parks said to a crowded house in the temple auditorium that their church choir was the best musical organization in the state of Oklahoma.

Lotus Jones attended high school at Boley, Oklahoma, and graduated in 1914. Shortly after graduating from high school he bought a theater, operating it until 1916. He took his two years of pre-medical training at Langston University (Oklahoma State School) finishing in 1920. Finished Meharry Medical College, Nashville, Tennessee, in 1924, maintaining an average of 93-plus for the four years, which is the third highest grade made in the class.

Lotus is a member of the Phi Beta Sigma fraternity. Married Lyla C. Watson of Ardmore, Oklahoma, February 4, 1924, in Nashville, Tennessee. Started the practice of medicine in Cleveland, Ohio, in 1925. Lotus, Jr., was born to this union November

12, 1929. Mrs. Lotus Jones taught music in Ardmore, Oklahoma, high school and Langston University, also Luther Olsla High School. She was a former pupil of his mother, Mayme, while in Boley. Finished at Chicago Music College in 1922.

Claude B. Jones took two years work in high school in Boley. His preparatory college work in Oklahoma University, thence to Wilberforce.

Claude is a born musician and is known throughout the country as the trombone king, is said to have no equal on the instrument in the United States. He married Miss Alma Thomas, senior co-ed of the University of Michigan, in 1927. He is at present with the Fletcher Henderson Orchestra of New York. This famous Negro orchestra has been playing under steady contract at the Roseland Ball Room in New York on Broadway for several years. This orchestra is reputed to be the best orchestra in the country.

Our first year under our firm name was a very successful one. Our patrons were mixed between the races, which means besides my own people, the English, white Americans, and foreigners from many lands. This year 1888 was a fruitful one, the mines worked almost full time. The men paid their bills promptly. I cannot agree with those people who say that the ordinary citizen is dishonest, and will not pay his debts if he can get around them. My experience covering a period of more than 40 years will not allow me to agree with that statement. I am rather inclined to the opinion that 95% of the people are honest and will pay if they can secure employment commensurate with their living expenses.

The next year we were enriched by the birth of our second girl, Ethel Mae. This year was noted for its sharp political contest as relates to this village. The races were about equally divided and each wanted to rule. While the contest was sharp they were friendly and never left any noticeable sore spots. In time the Negro population outnumbered the whites, and instead of taking every thing as they could have done they divided the offices with their white brothers and by so doing we have kept up a relationship akin to love.

I never entered into a contest for an elective municipal office, though often solicited. I have acted as central committeeman and have served for years as county executive committeeman, have had the honor of being elected to county, judicial, congressional, and state conventions. Contact with this class gave me a wide acquaintance which has been helpful to me all through the years. The next child that came to our family was Hazel, a beautiful, healthy child showing evidence of a high grade of intelligence. Because of this fact the old lady who stayed with us at this time said that we would not raise her. I was in Wheeling with Flem and Charlie to attend the first commencement held by McHenry, while there a message came calling me home at once. I reached home just in time to see the breath leave her little body.

John L., Jr., was born March 8th, 1891. Our next and last child, Earl R., was born March 5th, 1893. His first visit was with his mother to the World's Fair the same year. They visited Cleveland and went to the Fair with Mrs. W. D. Wright and her daughter, Edith, who was about the same age as Earl. I went to the Fair with Wm. Harris, John Walker, Theo. Johnson, Charlie and Tommie joined us there, we had more pleasure with each other than at the Fair. I am the only survivor of this group.

At the electoral college in Washington Court House, Ohio, I was elected to represent the Ohio annual conference at the quadrennial meeting of the A.M.E. church held in Philadelphia, Pennsylvania. At this meeting I met some of the strong men of our church and race. Learned much from contact with them and received lasting inspiration. I had the honor of assisting in the election of three Bishops, Lee, Handy, and Saulter. Heard some of our most renowned orators including Dr. ------ from Africa, who also was the manager of our coffee plantation there. We were in Philadelphia one month and before returning home I made a trip to New York along with the Rev. A. J. Means, who had lived in the city and could point out the places of interest. When a boy I read in the old Cincinnati *Commercial* about the government of Egypt donating Cleopatra's Needle to the U.S.A. The Needle was brought to this country on a raft and set up in New York's Central Park. I wanted to see this monument above anything in the city. We took in the zoo and then walked for 10 blocks until we reached the Needle. My dream came true, I saw the Needle, climbed over the railing and touched it, to do so was to place ones self subject to being fined, but I was willing to pay a small fine to have the pleasure of touching this ancient monument. We next went through the tenement district, then to Brooklyn Bridge, then Castle Garden, then to the ferry in time to see our horizon at our feet. We came back to Philadelphia and spent another week before returning home. I was anxious to mingle again with my family and friends and yet reluctant to come away from that higher life with which we were surrounded. I have never since enjoyed such an atmosphere. Sometimes it seemed that Heaven had come down to dwell among men. One day while in Philadelphia. I lost my pocket book containing $40.00. When I went to our temporary post office next day and called for my mail the postmaster gave me the book with the money intact. Of course I was very happy though I had sent to my wife to send more money which she did in a short time.

In this year we had another lull in the coal trade in this valley we had eleven months of rest from labor. Many business men went into bankruptcy, and many more were on the verge, including myself. My shelves were depleted, and looked very much like a cyclone had passed through.

I was many months behind with my bills. Ira Bell, one of my regular salesmen, came into my place on his regular trip and insisted upon me buying a bill of goods from him, I told him that I was so far behind that his house would not ship any more to me and that I could not blame them. He insisted and assured me that they would ship. I gave him a small order but knew that they would not ship. In a couple of days I had a letter from the house stating that they would have to turn down my order as they did not see any signs of resumption of business in this territory, and while they regretted to have to do so yet the situation compelled it. In answer I told them that I did not blame them and felt no ill will toward them for turning down my order, and that the outlook for resumption of business looked dark. Some day the sun will shine and this dark night will be forgotten. I will be here and pay you the last farthing. The next day I received a return letter from them saying, that my order had gone forward, and that hereafter my orders would be shipped promptly. The letter was closed by saying, that any man who would write such a letter as mine would never beat anyone out of anything. This happened 30 years ago, and we are still substantial friends.

Talk about hard times, old timers tell you that the present times are nothing as compared with the last half of the Cleveland administration. All through Southeastern Ohio the people were forced to call on the governor for aid. At a mass meeting of miners the writer was elected as a single delegate to go to Columbus and wait on Governor McKinley in the interest of the miners of this district. This great and good man was touched by the appeal. He called in his right-hand man, Mr. Round, canal commissioner, and had a car of provisions being loaded for Nelsonville, Ohio, switched to Rendville, Ohio. Then the governor asked me to come back to his office after dinner that the press might have an interview with me. I returned at one o'clock and was interviewed by about ten reporters. The next morning all of the papers carried my version of the actual conditions in this section. We had messages from individuals and welfare societies from as far east as Boston, Massachusetts, asking if we could use children's and women's clothing. We wired acceptance and they were shipped promptly. These conditions lasted until the end of the campaign of 1896. Money was tight, the government was forced to sell bonds to meet the running expenses of the government. A free trade bill passed in the lower house, but failed in the upper house. Bryan's cross of gold and his 16-to-1 was on every tongue, free silver and Coin's financial school seemed to have captured the nation, Bryan's election seemed reasonably certain. The Republicans woke up a few weeks before the election, when the tide turned in favor of the gold standard and McKinley was elected president over William Jennings Bryan.[20]

Faithful party workers began to scramble for places, held for four years by the faithful Democrats. I was a candidate for the appointment of the post office at this place. I had opposition in the person of Mr. Geo. P. Tharp. Mr. Tharp made a fight but a losing one as I had every member of the county committee pulling for me. I had been a party worker for years and the party was glad of the opportunity to secure my appointment.

John A. Birkimer, Shelly McDonald, Judge Frank A. Kelly, Judge Jas. Johnson, Samuel Pasco and others shall have my everlasting gratitude for their unselfish support. Together with Gen. Charles Grosvenor they smashed the icons of prejudice and let down the bars allowing me a place of honor and trust. Glorious iconoclast, noble and true, I would not have been here for 33 years were it not for you.

I received my commission July 1st, 1897. Knowing that I would be appointed, I was allowed through the kindness of Mr. Charles Hearing, my predecessor, to acquaint myself with the work and have access to the postal laws and regulations. When the time came for me to take over the office I was well prepared. My wife was sworn in for deputy and between us took care of the store and office.

Zenobia took the Boxwell examination at 12 and represented her class at the county commencement held in the Smith opera house, New Lexington. She was the last to speak and if judged from the deafening applause was very highly esteemed. The ladies threw up their hats and many rushed to the platform to shower their congratulations. After finishing her course in the N. and I. school at Institute, West Virginia, 1901, she came home and was of much service to us at the time of the big fire in October of that year. The fire originated in a house about one-half block from us and continued to burn until 16 houses were consumed, including our home, store and office. We saved most of our furniture and store equipment. It was very sad to see men and women the next morning standing in groups weeping. Some of them had lost their all, many refused to carry insurance on account of the high rate and it would seem at this rate that weeping was in order.

Our office cabinet had been removed to a side street and for several days we kept the mail going from that convenient location.

I sent my family, excluding Zenobia, to Cleveland, we found a house also a room for the office and were soon in position to have the family come back home so as to start the children back to school. Next day after the fire Charley and McHenry came down and offered us financial assistance, W. B. Wright came down from Cleveland, and said to me, "I brought along my check book." F. C. Martin of the Saml Stevens Grocery Co., of Columbus, came down to render any assistance that we might need, even to building. W. W. Harper of Zanesville, made the same offer. Fortunately I was in a position to go through on my own account, but was strengthened by those friendly proffers. We entered into a contract with Mr. Frank Childs of New Lexington, a contractor and builder, who threw on a force of men and had our building ready by Christmas. We stocked up with a nice clean supply of goods. Our room was new, clean, light, and attractive. Our patronage was all that could be desired, two of the children were large enough to help and with Mrs. Jones and myself we were kept busy between the store and office. At the end of the year we had forgotten that we ever had a fire.

On account of the work and strain connected with my work at this time, I had a nervous breakdown which lasted five years. I was able to direct the work, but unable to lift any weight without having to take [to] my bed. Zenobia, was attending school at Denison University. A young man by the name of W. A. Payne was attending the same school and when he received his degree they married and went at once to Pasadena, California, where he was employed as secretary of the Pacific Land Co. They incorporated a town and formed a colony at which time the Payne family moved there. Mr. Payne (like my father at South Point, Ohio) found that he was not intended for pioneer life, and answered the call back to the school room. I have known him from boyhood and never knew him to do anything but teach school, attend associations, Sabbath school conventions, educational meetings and try to play ball. They have eight children, all are in school. Zenobia has been teaching for six or seven years, besides she finds time to work among the unfortunate poor and needy. The night is never too inclement for her to go to those who need encouragement or spiritual advice. She is not a fanatic, but her hobby is the Bible and practical Christianity.

The family are living in El Centro, California, where Mr. Payne has charge of a large school for Negroes and Mexicans. Octavia, the oldest daughter, will receive her degrees in June from the University of Southern California. Mr. Payne received his Master's from this school. Ethel finished the grade school at twelve, attended Corning High School four years and after graduation

51

took a special course in domestic art at Institute, West Virginia, continuing her studies in Chicago University and Columbia University, New York City. She was first employed at St. Paul, an Episcopal school at Lawrenceville, Virginia. After teaching three years she resigned to take work in the home school. Tiring of grade teaching she applied for work at Wilberforce University, securing the appointment. She installed domestic art there. After teaching at Wilberforce for three years she resigned to marry H. G. Tolliver, of New Haven, Connecticut. H. G. was a young lawyer, graduate of Yale Law School, had a large clientele, was an alderman for eight years and corporation counsel of the city. He died while mowing his lawn in June, 1927. He left besides a widow, four children. Harry was very popular with all classes. I never saw strong men break down and weep as they did over the death of Harry. On the day of his funeral the flag was lowered to half mast, street car service was suspended, 150 city officials led by the Mayor marched in the funeral procession.

Ethel is equally popular. The best of the citizens insisted upon her remaining in the city with the promise of securing her a position in the city government. The promise was made good and she is employed by the city with a satisfactory salary attachment.

John was an earnest student from the time he entered school until the last. He was the only one of his race in a large class in the Corning High School. He was Valedictorian of the class, and after he had made his oration he had to make his class day oration by request. The year following graduation from Corning he went to Oberlin College. He was just 19 and insisted on going to work so as to help himself through college. He went to Oklahoma, and secured a school, taught one year then took the civil service examination for rural carrier out of the Boley office. He bought two fine horses for this work. A disease broke out among the horses in that place, and both died. He then bought a Ford car for use on his route. He secured a leave of absence for one month so as to try work as railroad clerk, his route was from Kansas City to some terminal in Texas. He did not like that work and returned back to his old position. He married Miss George E. Haynes. One daughter blessed this union. Gathered up in this time a nice little bunch of money, made a hasty investment and lost all. Quit Boley and moved to Kansas City during the World War, held a position in the terminal post office there in charge of the Arizona State mail. This was a good position but only lasted until the holder returned from overseas.

He was employed as principal of the school in Olathe, Kansas. The next year he was employed in the school at Topeka, Kansas. The next year attended college in the University of Kansas.

Anxious to finish his college work, came home and entered Ohio State University. In reach of his degree for which he had striven for years he took sick, came home as we thought for a short time, but as time passed it became evident that his trouble was serious. We employed several doctors from Columbus, Zanesville, and Charleston, West Virginia. For a short while he seemed to improve and gained 14 pounds. I never saw him looking better, he was the picture of health, had dressed for church, and had been joking with his mother, when all at once he began to bleed profusely, and before I could get to the telephone to call a doctor he passed away.

The passing of John was the greatest shock that ever befell our family. His friends as well were slow to believe the news. He never looked better, his future never seemed more promising than on this fatal Sunday evening. When I looked down upon his lifeless perfect body I thought of David when his son, Absolem died and said in my heart, "O John, my son, my son, would God I had died for thee, O John, my son, my son."

Earl, the youngest one of this division of the family, finished the grades in the Rendville school, and made two years in Corning High School. Earl learned rapidly, had a very alert mind, had no trouble in keeping up with his class, but was not over-ambitious and for that reason gave up his high school work with the second year. He worked in the store the next year and finally concluded to go back to school. He took up an industrial course in Wilberforce University, after which he returned home and took up work with us in the store, remaining until called to arms in 1917.

Before going to the war he married Miss Viola Page. They have three very interesting children. Our kinsmen have engaged in every war for the perpetuity of this country with the single exception of 1812, we can find no data for this war. The archives at Washington, DC, give mute evidence of the activities of Uncle John Ailstock who followed the fortunes of George Washington and was with his little freezing, hungry army at Valley Forge. Many were in the Civil War, also the Spanish-American War.

In the World War, waged to make this country a better place in which to live, we sent two, one of them was Earl. He enlisted by induction at Camp Meade, Maryland. Was in camp two months then off for France. Served in the 351st Field Artillery, Battery F. Saw service on the front in a heated engagement for 14 days, 12 kilometers out of Metz, in the Meuse Sector. This was the first time that Negro soldiers were ever allowed to handle heavy ordinance and history says that they behaved nicely.

We have traced briefly the genealogy of the Jones family covering a period of one hundred and seventy-seven years. As a family we have little to boast of in the way of accomplishments, we take pride only in the fact that we are a family of eugenics or well born, coming from a pure blood strain, from a sparkling flowing fountain. We should feel grateful to our fathers who bequeathed to us this splendid heritage of health of body and mind. This seems to have been a secret compact, and we should see to it that this compact is not broken. This we owe to our family, our government and to our God.

HISTORY OF THE JONES FAMILY

NOTES

1. Although the story of the progenitor of the Jones family never being a slave is possible, it is more likely that Jones family ancestors were freed from slavery prior to the memories of John Jones's parents. A note found in Jackson's *Free Negro Labor and Property Holders in Virginia 1830-1860*, p. 125 (1942), offers a possible lead: In 1800 William Jones of Henrico County, Virginia, liberated 31 slaves and settled them on land he called Jonestown. (See Deed Bk. 6, p. 440, *Henrico County Deeds*.) Although three Reuben Joneses are listed in Woodson's *Free Negro Heads of Families in the United States in 1830*, one was in North Carolina, one was in Randolph County, Virginia, and one was in Henrico County, Virginia. Both of the Virginia Reuben Joneses were aged 36-55, which is appropriate for Joseph Jones's father. Both were characterized as mulatto. The Randolph County man had six in his household and the Henrico County man had eight people under his roof. Although the evidence is not conclusive, it is probably safe to say that the Reuben Jones in question was the Henrico County man. There are two reasons for this: 1) John Jones's account puts the number in the family at eight, and 2) places them in Richmond before coming to Ohio. [For an illuminating account of the situation of antebellum African-Americans, read Carter G. Woodson's introduction to his 1925 look at free blacks in 1830.]

By 1840 Reuben Jones was living in Raccoon Township, Gallia County, Ohio (*1840 Federal Census, Gallia Co., OH*, p. 17). Since the 1840 census listed only the name of the head of the household (Reuben Jones in this instance), it is not possible to say with certainty who the other members of the household were. The male between the ages of 55 and 100 would surely have been

Reuben, and the male between the ages of 10 and 24 was most likely Joseph. Joseph's birth year is calculated from later censuses as 1825 (*1850 Federal Census, Lawrence Co., OH*, p. 881; and *1860 Federal Census, Gallia Co., OH*, p. 502). He would, thus, fit the age category of the only other male in Reuben's household. If Joseph did come to Ohio at age 13 (as his son writes in *History of the Jones Family*), the family would have arrived about 1838. The account given in the memorial has Joseph coming with his parents to Ohio in 1833.

If Reuben Jones was one of the 31 slaves liberated in Henrico County in 1800, he would have been born a slave. If he were 55 in 1840, he would have been old enough to have remembered slavery. In fact, the 1850 census provides his age as 61 which makes his birth year as 1789 (*1850 Federal Census, Lawrence Co., OH*, p. 88). Perhaps he and his wife preferred to weave a tale rather than have the family bear the stigma of slavery.

Five females were also in the household. One may well have been Mrs. Jones, as her age was between 36 and 55. The youngest was between the ages of 10 and 16 and all of the other three females in Reuben's household were between the ages of 10 and 24. According to John L. Jones's account, the names of two daughters were Mary and Martha. The census entry would indicate the possibility of two other daughters. The 1850 census entry for Reuben's household has a Margaret Jones, born in Virginia, who was likely the 10-to-16-year old in the 1840 census, and possibly another daughter. The oldest son, John, was apparently on his own in 1840.

The Reuben Jones family was one of only two families in Raccoon Township identified as "free colored persons" in 1840. The other family was that of William Field.

2. In the memorial to James McHenry Jones (reprinted here) is the comment that Reuben's wife was Elizabeth Ailstock, the youngest daughter of six children. Her father was Joseph Ailstock, son of an Englishman. He was supposed to have followed George Washington from Boston to Yorktown. His wife was half Indian.

3. The account of Joseph's coming to Ohio is different from that offered in *In Memoriam*. There it states that Joseph came with his parents in 1833 and settled near Gallipolis. Refer to Note 1 for further elaboration.

4. The marriage date of 1842 is given in James McHenry's memorial. Joseph and Temperance's marriage is recorded in *Lawrence Co., OH, Marriage Book 4*, p. 90, as 16 Nov 1847. Temperance's maiden name was Reid.

Joseph and Temperance appear in the 1850 federal census for Fayette Township, Lawrence County, Ohio (p. 881) with their one-year old son, William H. According to their entry they were both born in Ohio 25 years before; however, this is probably not accurate. Joseph and Temperance also appeared in the 1860 federal census (*Gallia County, Ohio, Gallipolis Township*, p. 502). Joseph's age is given as 35 and his place of birth as Virginia; this is probably accurate. Temperance's age is given as 25, but since it was also given as 25 in 1850, her age is in question. Indications from *The History of the Jones Family* show that she was probably quite young when she married, and that she was born 15 May 1824. It is therefore likely that she was 26 in 1850. Perhaps Temperance preferred to be thought of as younger.

According to the memorial, Temperance's mother brought her to Lawrence County, Ohio, from Kentucky in 1802, and James McHenry Jones spent his early boyhood on his grandmother's farm in Lawrence County before removing to New Richmond, Ohio. Temperance would not have been old enough to have been brought to Ohio in 1802. The farm James McHenry may have recalled could have been that of William and Nancy Reed. They were living next door to Joseph and Temperance in 1850 in Lawrence County and would have been Temperance's parents. William, age 50 in 1850, was born in Kentucky according to the census entry. This means that it may have been William who was brought to Ohio by his mother in 1802 from Kentucky.

The Reed family, as enumerated in the 1850 census, corresponds with John L. Jones's account. Mary was 16 years old; Rosetta was 12. John, who became a boatman, was only 6 in 1850. William H. was 5; and James H. was only 2 years old; Samuel and George were not listed. They could have been older and already removed from the household (*1850 Federal Census, Lawrence Co., OH*, p. 881).

5. John L. Jones is featured in *The Book of Perry County: An Historic Industrial Portfolio* (1910). At the time Jones was the postmaster of Rendville. According to this account he was born in Meigs County, Ohio, 13 July 1857 and came to Rendville in 1881. Having worked in the mines, organized and, eventually, purchased the cooperative store, he was in 1909 the proprietor of

a general store in Rendville. An active Republican, he was appointed to his postmaster position in 1897 by then-President, William McKinley. He had served on the school board and was a council member. He was a Methodist and a member of the Knights of Pythias. He married Sadie D. Broadis of Columbus in 1887. They had four children. The biography ended with this statement: "Mr. Jones has made a careful official and has the confidence of all who know him."

According to his death certificate, John L. Jones died in El Centro, Imperial County, California, 13 May 1938 near or at the home of his daughter, Zenobia. Widowed, he had lived in California for eight years. Zenobia gave his birthplace as New Richmond, Ohio. She gave his mother's birthplace as Burlington, Ohio. Burial was in Evergreen Cemetery near El Centro, California. Heart trouble appeared to be the cause of death.

6. Census records would indicate that the parents came to Ohio much earlier than Jones's narration implies (see the family chart for elaboration). Of course, he had this information secondhand and probably did not recall his grandparents.

7. In 1850 Reuben Jones was living in Lawrence County, Ohio, and his household included Robert Love, age 25, and Nancy Love, age 2. Also in the household were Margaret Jones, age 21, and Roxa Scott, age 15 (*1850 Federal Census, Fayette Twp, Lawrence Co., OH*, p. 88). Margaret could have been the youngest daughter of Reuben Jones. In 1840 he had a female in his household aged 10-16. This could have been Margaret. She could have married Robert Love and had the two children mentioned by John L. Jones. Margaret was born in Virginia as was Robert Love.

8. According to the memorial, James (Mc)Henry Jones was born 28 Aug 1859 in Gallipolis, Ohio.

9. Reuben's 1850 household (according to the federal census) did not include a woman who could have been his wife. Neither did Joseph's household. It would appear that Mrs. Jones died before 1850 rather than in 1859 as John L. Jones recounts. Reuben may, indeed, have died about then. He does not appear in the 1860 census.

10. Joseph's early career on the river and his several homes along the Ohio River point to his involvement in the Underground Railroad for many years. Horton (1993) points out that black boatmen had a long history of carrying news between free and runaway blacks in the North to their relatives and friends still held in slavery in the South. Boatmen were often directly responsible for aiding escapes and had long worked as conductors on the Railroad. Horton's research indicates that the Underground Railroad was an informal and loose-knit activity staffed mostly by blacks and only sometimes by whites. Often these people had a personal connection to the enslaved, and free blacks were active at all levels of the Underground.

Fugitives usually had to make the first, hazardous portion of their escapes on their own. Those lucky enough to reach a free state then depended on the Underground. Those areas along the Ohio River where Joseph lived were first stops on the Railroad.

11. Beulah A. Johnson of Gallipolis, a pioneer in researching local black history, searched the newspapers for the time and found articles corroborating Jones's account of the strained relations between soldiers, white townspeople and black townspeople. Page 2 of *The Gallipolis Journal* of 27 Nov 1862 had two stories. The first item:

Our town was thrown into a fever of excitement a few evenings since, in consequence of a report that a soldier had been struck in the head with an iron dray pin, in the hand of a Negro, and killed. The Negro was lodged in jail. A crowd of soldiers and some citizens who were at this time peculiarly zealous against a nigger, assembled at the jail and threatened to take him by force and hang him. They were armed with sabers, knives, pistols and muskets. The Negro was taken in charge by Lieutenant Gilman of the "Guards" and brought before Capt. Smith, commander of the post.

The facts proven, the soldier was still alive and able for his whiskey as usual. He had been hospitalized for some time and the day before the affray was in the guard house for drunkenness.

On his release from the guard house he took occasion to go over on 3rd St. and enter the home of a Negro family behaving most outrageously and exhibiting his person in the most indecent manner. Attempting to lay hands on an aged Negro woman, her grandson picked up a hoop-pole and dislocated the jaw of the soldier.

Rumor changed the hoop-pole to an iron dray pin and the dislocated jaw into the first stage of death.

The fact that the blow was given by a "damned nigger" was enough to seal his doom for simply defending his aged grandmother from the ruffian attacks of a drunken soldier. The second article:

Our town was again thrown into excitement Monday evening by another riot between some men of Capt. Leaper's Cavalry Co. and some Negroes in the upper end of town. And as usual the fracas ended in discomfiture of the Negroes but not until one of the Cavalry men received a severe wound in the arm from a revolver in the hands of one of the Negroes. How it began we neither know or care. That it took place in "Africa" is an indication that the Cavalry was not on its own ground.

It seems passing strange that this should be allowed but so it is whether because it is impossible for the officer to restrain his men or the fault of the men themselves it is hard to say.

"General Whiskey" was at the bottom of it all. Capt. Leaper very soon knocked the bottom out of Gen. Whiskey but whether at his own expense or at the cost of the owners remain to be seen. It is well that this question be settled at once.

This hue and cry against the Negroes of Gallipolis will avail but little. There is a limit to it beyond which men of sense will not go. If because one Negro misbehaves the whole colored population are to be hunted down like wild beasts, the sober judgment of men heretofore unfriendly to the Negro will revolt against it.

Abraham Lincoln officially freed the slaves 1 Jan 1863, but he issued the Emancipation Proclamation on 22 September 1862. The incidents described by the sympathetic Gallipolis newspaper occurred between these two dates. The impending changes may have added to tensions during the war period.

The blacks of Gallia County, Ohio lost no time in celebrating their southern cousins' independence. Their Emancipation Day celebration began September 22, 1863, a year after the Proclamation, and has continued ever since with the exception of 1887 when times were particularly hard. The Gallia County Emancipation Day Celebration is the oldest continuous such one in the country (Fleischman, 1993).

Research by Sara Johnson Davis, carrying on the tradition after
her mother's death in 1991, showed that the Emancipation
celebrations had drawn crowds as large as 7,000 which would
overwhelm modern Gallipolis. Events included sack races, greasy
pole climbs, baseball, and dancing. Now, fewer people come
(although the crowds have been growing larger than they were a
few decades ago) and present day activities include an art show,
a history display, children's games, and church services. Whereas
old time crowds were comprised primarily of those who had left
to seek work in urban areas such as Dayton, the modern celebration hosts not only townspeople and those returning home but also
African-Americans drawn by their interest in their roots and their
culture. Many of these people have no connection to Gallipolis
other than their interest in this rather remarkable celebration
(Fleischman, 1993).

12. Interest in the historical and sociological background of
African-American families was sparked during the Civil Rights
movement of the 1950s and 1960s. An outcome of this interest was
Daniel Moynihan's 1965 report *The Negro Family: The Case
for National Action* (U.S. Department of Labor, Washington:
Government Printing Office), which drew on standard works of
the 1930s and 1940s that promoted the notion that African-
American families were predominately matriarchal and that this
condition, begun during slavery, persisted throughout the history
of Africans in America. Moynihan laid the blame for the disinte-
gration of the "ghetto black family" at the feet of this matriarchal
system. Although social scientists disagreed, none looked at the
crucial issue that was passed over by the earlier works and the
Moynihan report: that of the condition of African-American
families from 1875-1915 when most urban black communities
began. Lammermeier in a 1973 study addressed that crucial issue.
He used census information from 1850 through 1880 to analyze the
structure of black families. His findings show that, contrary to
earlier assumptions, the matriarchal system established of necessity during slavery, dissolved after the Civil War. African-American families in the latter part of the 19th century were organized
in the normal patriarchal structure. The Jones family and other
African-American families discussed in the book, by clearly
illustrating this situation, provide very nice case studies of
African-American family life of the period.

13. Professor T. J. Furguson/Ferguson, pastor of the newly organized Free Will Baptist Church in Pomeroy in the latter quarter of the 19th century was "late of Enterprise Academy, Albany," according to the memorial to James McHenry Jones. James McHenry studied with Ferguson—probably during his tenure in Pomeroy. *In Memoriam* states that James taught at the Enterprise Academy. According to Tribe (1969) "a Mr. Jones" *was* a teacher at the Academy, a special institution in the history of the education of African-Americans.

About 1847 the Ichabod Lewis family arrived in Albany and the daughter, Lamira, begin teaching classes in their home. The classes were such a success that Lamira's brother, William, who had attended Oberlin College (a seat of abolitionist activities), bought a lot, built a school house, and opened the Lewis Academy to any student without regard to race or sex. This, too, was a success. Another building was built and by 1850 some Albany residents organized a stock company which purchased controlling interest in the Lewis Academy. It was reorganized and renamed the Albany Manual Labor Academy. Students who could not afford tuition could work for the school to finance their education. Students of any race or sex continued to be admitted.

No doubt as a consequence of the liberal attitudes fostered by the Albany Manual Labor Academy, the African-American population of Albany increased from four in 1850 to 174 in 1860. However, by 1862 the Albany Manual Labor Academy was forced to close because of the lack of funds. Its successor, the Atwood Institute, refused admission to blacks. The black citizens of Albany, as a consequence, formed their own school in 1863 (Tribe, 1969).

The Enterprise Academy was the first school owned and operated by blacks (Wright, 1976). The school's 1864 constitution states that the decision to restrict ownership to "colored persons" was a result of the need to "demonstrate the capacity of colored men to originate and successfully manage such a school. . . ." A circular "To the Friends of the Colored People" (Albany, Athens County, Ohio, 14 March 1864) further proclaims similar sentiments expressed in a stronger manner. T. J. Ferguson/Furguson, as President of the Board of Trustees, signed the circular.

An advertisement in the *Colored Citizen* (Cincinnati) for 19 May 1866 stated that the fall term was to begin September 6. The 60 students were taught by the Rev. John P. Bowles, Principal, and Miss Addie Goings. Tuition in the primary department was $3.00

and $4.50 in the academic department. Music and language was extra.

By the fall of 1874 Prof. W.S. Scarborough of Oberlin College arrived to teach at the Albany Enterprise Academy (*Athens Messenger*, 19 Nov 1874). He joined Prof. John Bowles, Jr., to teach only 30 students (*Athens Messenger*, 24 Dec 1874). A few years later in 1877 only 23 students attended classes and only one instructor was needed (U.S. Report, 1877-1887). By 1879, however, prospects looked brighter for the Academy as the U.S. Report for 1877-1887 listed 64 students and four instructors. Thereafter the number of students remained between 58-65 with three instructors.

Money was always a problem for the Albany Enterprise Academy, no doubt due to its attitude of education for all. In 1866 the trustees asked the public to provide 200 scholarships at $50 each, which would enable the holders to attend school for five years, because "hundreds, by the war, have been forced out from Virginia and Kentucky, and now reside in the vicinity of this school" . . . and "to become good citizens they must be educated" (*Colored Citizen*, 19 May 1866). Consequently, even though the numbers of students remained stable from 1879 to 1886, the students were poor. In 1886 Principal Thomas J. Furguson, resigned due to illness and the Albany Enterprise Academy closed its doors (Tribe, 1969).

Among the distinguished alumni of the Albany Enterprise Academy were Olivia Davidson, the second wife of Booker T. Washington, who worked alongside her husband at Tuskegee Institute, and her brother, Andrew Jackson Davidson, who practiced law in Athens, Ohio. Edwin Berry owned a hotel in Athens known nationally for its fine accommodations open to persons of any race. Milton M. Holland, born in Texas, came to Albany for an education. He was one of the first group of twelve blacks to be awarded the Medal of Honor for his service in the Union Army. His older brother, William H. Holland, served in the Texas state senate (Tribe, 1969).

14. *In Memoriam* has a more elaborate version of James McHenry's integration of Pomeroy High School. At the time, blacks were excluded from Ohio public schools by the "Black Laws" which began with the Ohio Constitution of 1802, giving white males the right to vote. [According to Shilling (1913), the petition to grant suffrage to the territory's male African-Americans was defeated by only one vote.] The Ordinance of 1787, of course, prohibited slavery in the Northwest Territory but allowed

for the return of fugitive slaves to their owners in the South. In 1804 Ohio passed a law prohibiting African-Americans from settling in the state unless they had papers proving their freedom. In 1807 the law was amended to include a $500 bond as a guarantee of "good behavior." [Shilling (1913) reported that no attempt was made to enforce the bond law until 1829 when the city of Cincinnati gave its African-American residents 30 days to comply. The effect was that one-half of the African-American population moved to Canada.] Moreover, the 1807 law stated that no African-American could testify against a white man in court, thus putting African-Americans at the mercy of unscrupulous whites. In 1829 a law was passed barring African-American children from the public schools. In 1831 African-Americans were prohibited from serving on juries. [Shilling (1913) drew the conclusion that Ohio's lack of welcome for African-Americans was due to the Southern sympathies of the southern portion of the state which controlled Ohio politics before the Civil War. As an example, Shilling noted that Cincinnati was dependent on the South for its economic growth before the coming of the railroad in the 1850s. Also, during the decade before the Civil War, the tobacco industry grew in southern Ohio. Due to the labor-intensive nature of tobacco growing, southern Ohio farmers hired slaves from neighboring Virginia and Kentucky to work in the fields. Even after most of the "Black Laws" were repealed, the Ohio legislature barely defeated a motion in 1850 to "discourage" African-American immigration by the narrow margin of 39 to 34.]

A tide of resentment against the "Black Laws" swelled in the 1830s and in 1849 some of the restrictions were lifted, including the prohibition against testifying in court. At the same time provisions were made for the education of African-American children at public expense, but law suits had to be filed before funds were forthcoming. A major step backward occurred in 1850 with the passing of the Fugitive Slave Law, but the Civil War brought about repeals of many of the Black Laws such as the right to vote (Sheeler, 1946). Schools, however, remained segregated by law.

Bishop Benjamin William Arnett of the African Methodist Episcopal Church, the first black state legislator to represent a predominately white constituency, was elected to the Ohio legislature from Greene County in 1885 (Ploski & Williams, 1992). Called the Arnett Bill after its promoter, the law which finally repealed the remaining "Black Laws" was passed 22 Feb 1887 (Laws of Ohio, 1887). Schools were no longer segregated by law.

Flem's and James's integration of Pomeroy High School occurred well before the "Black Laws" were repealed.

15. When Alex and John L. Jones went to Rendville they became part of a fascinating piece of history. Historian Herbert G. Gutman's influential monograph on the role of African-Americans in the early years of the United Mine Workers of America focuses on Richard L. Davis, a black Rendville miner. Davis, born a slave, according to Nelson (1986), in Roanoke, Virginia, worked in a tobacco factory until he was 17. Then, he migrated north through the coal fields of the New River. He arrived in Rendville the year after John Jones came.

While Jones wanted to educate his race, Davis wanted to organize them. Davis joined the UMW and became a union organizer and activist. In 1891 he was elected to the Executive Board of UMW District 6 (Ohio) and held the post for five years. In 1896 and, again, in 1897 Davis was elected to the National Executive Board of the UMW. It is thought that Davis was the only African-American to hold a national office in the UMW at such an early date although other members of his race were active in the union and often held offices at regional and local levels.

According to Gutman, black strike breakers were brought into the Hocking Valley Coal Region of which Rendville was a part in 1874-1875 but little is known about this event (p. 174). By 1880 when Alex Jones arrived, the dispute must have been settled and some agreement reached whereby black miners were encouraged to come but, according to Gutman's research, were assigned to one mine, Mine #3. Nelson's (1986) account reports that Colonel Rend recruited Irish, Welsh and English immigrants with no mining experience. They took one look and made hasty retreats. Rend, then, turned to the New River region of West Virginia and hired 100 black miners. They were not strike breakers, but they were hired with "sliding scale" contracts which meant that their wages shot up and down with the price of coal. Neighboring white mining towns saw the arrival of the black miners as a threat and marched several hundred strong into Rendville. The so-called "Corning War" ended when Governor Foster sent in the militia armed with a Gatling gun.

Davis's letters to the UMW *Journal* indicate that nearby mining towns such as Corning, Straitsville and Shawnee continued to be off limits to blacks. Davis reported that he and a group of white union officers left a restaurant in nearby Corning because the proprietor would not seat Davis.

The Knights of Labor was the earliest union in the Hocking Valley coal fields and, as Jones indicates, black miners joined quickly. Brier (1980) notes that interracial local assemblies of the Knights of Labor existed in the New River and Hocking Valley coal fields as early as 1880. A black assembly, #1935, was organized in 1882 in Rendville, the year Davis arrived in town. An interracial local was formed four years later. Leon Fink (1983) in his book on the Knights of Labor cites as an example of their most important push for political power in 1886 the election of a black miner as mayor of Rendville. This "black miner" was Isaiah S. Tuppins, the first black graduate of what became the Ohio State Medical School. He may have come to Rendville to work the mines, but Tuppins could hardly have been described as a "black miner" upon his election. In fact, his obituary in the Cleveland *Gazette* of 19 Jan 1889 does not mention mining. He came to Rendville as a physician. The *Gazette* notes that Tuppins was the first of his race to acquire the office of mayor in the Central and Eastern United States. He was re-elected and died during his second term. He was among those "progressive citizens" who helped organize the Miners' Cooperative Store of which John Jones was the manager. J. L. Jones was one of the eulogizers at the funeral in Xenia, Ohio.

Another was W. G. Clark who may have been the William *E*. Clark who wrote letters to the UMW *Journal* in 1893 and 1894 condemning racial prejudice. He was likely the same William Clark who, nine years later, was shot to death in his sleep by local police during a bitter West Virginia strike (Gutman, p. 171).

With the formation of the UMW in 1890 Davis turned his attention to the crucial issues of black participation, strike-breaking and racism within the union. Richard L. Davis wrote many letters to the UMW *Journal* as he had previously to the *National Labor Tribune* (see Brier, 1980). He also journeyed to the south to organize miners and had near-misses with death. As Charles Nelson put it in his article on Rendville "To be a union organizer in that era was dangerous enough; to be a black union organizer in the Deep South was nothing short of terrifying" (Nelson, 1986). In his letters Davis raged against "blacklegs" or scabs and insisted on a fair wage for every man, black or white. His insights into the working man's condition, and especially that of the black working man, are compelling. The gist of his thoughts is eloquently summed up by these remarks, "We boast of this being the home of the brave and the land of the free, but can you not see the deception of the thing? Now, let us have the truth. Is this not the land of the rich and the home of the slave?" (Gutman, pp. 167-168). Davis wrote this in a letter published by the UMW *Journal* in its 27 Oct 1892 issue. Gutman (1976) notes that this was less than three years before Booker T. Washington urged African-Americans at the Atlanta Exposition to take a "path of improvement derived from eighteenth-century individualist thought and devoid of a clear assessment of the realities shaped by a maturing industrial society." Gutman points out that Davis's letter concludes with language foreign to Washington's numerous admirers. Davis wrote: "Let us learn that an injury to one is the concern of all. Until we do learn this, we can hope for no better."

John L. Jones's views would seem to align more closely with those of Washington, but he certainly was given food for thought by activists such as Davis and Clark who lived and worked with him in Rendville. In fact, Davis probably lived just a few doors from Jones on Short Main Street in Rendville. The 1900 Federal Census has a Mary Davis, 34 year old widow with two small children, living just six doors away from the Jones family (p. 137 A). This was very probably Davis's family; Davis, himself died that year before the census was taken. It is possible that Jones, too, may have shared Davis's radical views, but by 1930 when he wrote his little book, he had mellowed. Davis might have had a quieter tone in his later years if he had lived. He, however, died in 1900, still a young man, of "lung fever."

Meanwhile Rendville prospered as a coal mining town until 1927 when a strike spelled the end. At the turn of the century Rendville had 13 bars, a hotel, a restaurant, four churches and 1,500 people (Dempsey, 1994). In 1994 Rendville has one church and 32 people (*Messenger*, 13 Mar 1994). The church, First Baptist, is, at 112 years, the oldest black church in Perry County (Dempsey, 1994), and the village is Ohio's smallest (*Messenger*, 13 Mar 1994).

16. James McHenry Jones was elected District Grand Master of the Odd Fellows Lodge in 1883, and Odd Fellows delegate to England in 1897 according to his memorial.

17. Jones's reference to the slump in coal business and most of the company moving west predates the 1894 account of labor agents for the Northern Pacific Coal Company in the state of Washington hiring Rendville Negro miners away *en masse* (Gutmann, p. 170). The great Hocking Valley coal strike of 1884-1885 may have provided the impetus for the 1887 date given here.

18. James McHenry Jones was elected president of West Virginia State College at Institute, in 1897—the same year he represented the Odd Fellows in England. He married for the second time to Elizabeth Moore of Cincinnati according to his memorial.

19. James McHenry Jones died 22 Sept 1909 of Bright's Disease and his funeral service was preached by Dr. I. V. Bryant according to his memorial. The Bryant family lived next door to the Reeds, parents of James's and John's mother, Temperance, and two doors away from Joseph and Temperance Jones in Lawrence County, Ohio, in 1850 (*1850 Federal Census, Lawrence Co., OH*, p. 881). Isaac Vinton Bryant was born in December of 1856 in Lawrence County. He attended the public schools in Burlington, Ohio, and the "Institute" at Ironton, Ohio. He began his preaching career in Cattletsburg, Kentucky, in 1879. He was pastor of churches in Ironton and Gallipolis, Ohio, and Charleston and Huntington, West Virginia, before taking charge of Walker Memorial Baptist Church in Washington, DC, in 1891. While there he took a medical course at Howard University but never pursued a medical career. Instead, he continued preaching and teaching. His simultaneous career as an educator began in Guyandotte, West Virginia, 1873-1877. He taught at schools where he had churches through the 19th century. In 1906 he returned to Huntington's First Baptist Church where he remained for over 16 years. Bryant gained a considerable reputation as an educator, political orator, and author, drawing large, white audiences to his sermons and lectures (Caldwell, 1923, and letter, 1922).

20. Not only was 1894 a bad year for Rendville but also for the whole country. The nation was in a deep depression. During this period Negro miners from Rendville were lured to Washington state where better conditions were promised in the coal fields of the Northern Pacific Coal Company (Gutman, p. 170). The Sunday Creek coal fields had already been suffering a depression of their own for the two previous years. The national depression drove the area into a situation so bad that William E. Clark in a letter to the UMW *Journal* wrote ". . . was this world of ours the hell we read about in the good book? If it is not, how can a man stand the punishment twice, and then live through eternity?" (Nelson, 1986).

J. McHenry Jones

IN MEMORIAM

J. McHenry Jones

BIOGRAPHICAL SKETCH OF J. McHENRY JONES

J. McHenry Jones was born in Gallipolis, Ohio, 28 August 1859. He came from one of the oldest families in Ohio, his maternal grandmother having been brought from Kentucky by her mother in 1802, and settled on a farm in Lawrence County. His paternal great-grandfather, Joseph Ailstock, the son of an Englishman who married an Indian squaw, followed the dubious fortunes of the great George Washington from the evacuation of Boston to the surrender of Yorktown.

Joseph Ailstock married a half-breed, and from this union six children were born. The youngest daughter, Elizabeth, married Reuben Jones, a free colored man, whose father came from Africa in his tenth year. His son, Joseph Jones, the father of the subject of this sketch, came with his parents to Ohio in 1833, and settled near Gallipolis. In 1842 he married Temperance Reid. J. McHenry Jones was the sixth son of a family of ten children. He spent his early boyhood with his grandmother on her farm in Lawrence County, later moving with his family to New Richmond. During his ninth year the family took up its residence at Pomeroy, Ohio, where he resumed his studies in the public school.

The demand for teachers being very great at that time, James, feeling himself better equipped than the majority of those engaged in the work, entered the profession during his sixteenth year and was placed in charge of a district school near Rutland. A year later, the Free Will Baptist church, of which he had been long a devout member licensed him to preach, a preparatory course in theology having been given him by Prof. T. J. Ferguson, late of Enterprise Academy, Albany.

James McHenry Jones early acquired the habit of reading. He did not neglect the games in which other boys of the little town engaged, but, unlike the majority of them, he had a craving for a higher education than was to be had in the graded schools of that period. He desired to enter the high school, but up to that time no colored boy or girl had attempted to enter the Pomeroy high school. At Albany, where he had taught the year before, a number of colored youth were pursuing the very course which he had mapped out for himself, and there he had made arrangements to go. In fact, he had purchased his ticket, when the thought occurred to him, while passing the high school building, to enter and ask to be enrolled. He acted upon the thought and, going directly to the principal's office, announced his intention of entering the school next day. The principal hesitated. To the city superintendent of schools, who was also present, young Jones turned and said, "The State of Ohio owes me an education; you must either allow me to enter this school or hire a special teacher to instruct me." He was admitted and graduated with the first honors of the class in 1882.[1]

It was shortly after his graduation that Mr. Jones saw in a colored newspaper, which fell into his hands, that a teacher was needed at Wheeling, West Virginia. He applied for the position and, having made the highest grade of the six applicants, was appointed. Here for sixteen years he labored patiently, building up his school, and increasing in personal usefulness and influence throughout his adopted state and those adjoining. During the early years of his residence at Wheeling he connected himself with Simpson Methodist Episcopal Church and remained an active, zealous member to the day of his death. The year 1888 witnessed his marriage to Miss Carrie Harrison, of Marietta, Ohio, with whom he lived an ideal life until her death, five years later.

Undoubtedly, as an educator the work of James McHenry Jones will be the more lasting, but it was in fraternal society circles that he gained the widest prominence. Mr. Jones entered the Grand United Order of Odd Fellows at eighteen years of age, a committee having waited upon his father to obtain permission. He was immediately made P.S., a position which he filled until he went to Wheeling. Matoka Lodge having sent in its charter, Mr. Jones became a member of Eureka Lodge at Wheeling. He attended the convention which met at Columbus, Ohio, previous to the organization of the District Lodge, and was elected Deputy Grand Master for the State, in 1883.

Having served in this office for two years, he resigned at Ironton and received a gold medal for distinguished services. He was elected District Grand Master at Zanesville, Ohio, in 1888. After serving three years, he again resigned. Two years before his election as District Grand Master, Mr. Jones became Grand Patriarchal Keeper. As District Grand Master of Ohio, J. McHenry Jones recommended sweeping changes in the government of the Order. Instead of the biennial convention, he advocated an Imperial Grand Lodge to meet triennially and to be composed of representatives from the District Grand Lodges. He would have the term District Grand Lodge abolished, and State Grand Lodges, with powers adequate to direct their internal affairs, substituted. He was also a strong advocate of Fraternal Insurance.

The Boston, Massachusetts, session of the Biennial Movable Convention witnessed his first nomination for the Grand Mastership. Declining, he stated why he could not be a candidate, and nominated another in his stead. Nevertheless he continued to occupy a prominent place in the councils of the Order, being elected unanimously at Indianapolis, Indiana, in 1896, the first Fraternal Delegate to bear the greetings of the Order in this country to the A.M.C. in England and represented his constituency at the A.M.C. at Bolton, England, Whit-week, 1897.

In 1902, at New Haven, Connecticut, the Grand United Order of Odd Fellows conferred upon him the highest honors at its disposal, electing him without opposition to the Grand Mastership. To this position he was again elected at Columbus, Ohio, two years later. Grand Master Jones took occasion in each of his biennial reports to again advocate State Grand Lodges as the unit of representation in the B.M.C. and he recommended the establishment of a national regalia department, and the founding of a fraternity bank.

While he never lost an opportunity to impress the necessity and importance of the adoption of these recommendations, he laid greater stress upon the Friendly Society Movement, an impression received from the trip to England, by which he hoped to unite for their mutual benefit all the Negro fraternal societies in America. His plan was to have each of the secret societies elect representatives for the formation of a general board which would work out a method by which funds could be raised to combat in Congress, the several State Legislatures, and before the courts all discriminatory measures and laws affecting the civil and political status of the Negro people. He often pointed out the ease with which an immense sum could be raised by taxing annually the members of fraternal societies each as little as five cents, but he did not live to see his proposition put into effect, although several organizations went so far as to appoint delegates for the purpose. However, his endowment proposition was adopted by several District Grand Lodges, and the national body elected him, in 1908, National Superintendent of Endowment with the power to establish an insurance department with the entire jurisdiction as its territory.

Mr. Jones was also a Mason and a Knight of Pythias, being in the latter organization a Past Chancellor, in the former, a Knight Templar.

When the presidency of the West Virginia Colored Institute, the leading institution in the state for the normal, industrial and agricultural education of Negro youth, became vacant in 1898, the position was offered to and accepted by Mr. Jones. With his wife who, as Miss Elizabeth Moore, of Cincinnati, Ohio, he had married in 1897, he removed to Institute September 21st of the following year.

At the time of his accession, the institution had only four buildings. At the time of his death there were seven, not taking into account a new barn, double greenhouse, and extensive additions to the academic and trades buildings, by which these two were more than doubled in size. During his incumbency the agricultural, military, commercial, and girls' science and arts departments were established; the mechanical department was enlarged by the addition of special teachers in blacksmithing, painting and house decorating, bricklaying and plastering, wheelwrighting, and mechanical and architectural drawing.[2]

For the instruction of girls, the industrial department had been broadened in scope to embrace dressmaking, millinery, cooking and laundering, for each of which a special teacher was employed. To carry on his work, he appeared before each session of the state legislature and was largely instrumental in securing the large appropriations which were made to the institution. That the male students might have the advantage of military instruction and equipment, he had introduced and passed a cadet bill which placed the West Virginia Colored Institute on par in that respect with the state university. That the graduates of the normal department might have the same privileges enjoyed by graduates of the white normal schools, President Jones guided through legislative channels a bill exempting from examination the holders of diplomas from his institution.

To keep in touch with the latest educational methods he did special work at the University of Michigan and pursued several reading courses. The institution over which he presided was gradually coming into national prominence, and its head was gaining recognition as a factor in educational circles beyond the boundaries of the state. To this recognition his ventures in literature contributed no small part.

He wrote a novel in 1890, but the publishing house having the manuscript failed, and the story, *A Strange Transformation*, was afterwards misplaced. Mr. Jones published at his own expense a story called, *Hearts of Gold*, a splendid addition to Afro-

American literature. He believed that his race had grown weary of reading white men's stories about "Uncle Toms" of the race and would welcome a story of the Negro as a man who feels, eats, talks, loves, and hates much like any other American.[3]

The cordial spirit with which *Hearts of Gold* was received, was the best indication of the author's judgment as expressed above, and its dramatization added to his reputation in the field of letters. A later contribution to literature was *The Bluvaynes*, a novel, arrangement for the publishing of which was about completed at the time of his death. Letters describing his travels in England, Scotland, Wales and France were published in the Odd Fellows *Journal* and received favorable comments from many persons of note.

Mr. Jones was a lecturer in frequent demand, and, at his demise, had appeared before many audiences in that capacity. His most popular subjects were: "The Triple Tie," "The Negro Problem Solved," "Don't—Danger Signals," "Is the Good Time Coming," "The Silent Voter of the Silent South," "Frederick Douglass," and "Abraham Lincoln."

On the stump he was equally popular and in as much demand. His was a familiar figure in every state convention since 1888, when, business having been suspended, Mr. Jones was invited to make an address. He canvassed the state for Harrison and Morton and took part frequently in national and congressional campaigns in Ohio. As an orator his voice was raised in defense of the principles of the Republican party in Virginia and Pennsylvania, as well as in the states of his nativity and adoption.[4]

J. McHenry Jones was, then, a worthy recipient of the honorary degree of Master of Arts which Shaw and Wilberforce Universities conferred upon him, and he bore with no less distinction the doctorate of Literature from Rust University. The Epworth League acknowledged and recognized his ability as an orator and educator when he was chosen as one of the speakers for the international convention at Seattle, Washington, in July, 1909. Here just as he did when representing the Odd Fellows in England, and his race on numerous other occasions, he acquitted himself with credit.

On the evening of September 22nd, 1909, after an illness of two months, J. McHenry Jones died of Bright's disease. Surrounded by his loving wife, grief-stricken brothers and a few sorrowing friends he went to his reward as calmly as a little child lies down to sleep.

Of the family there survived Alex J., John L., Flem B. and Charles E. Jones, brothers.

The remains were interred at Institute where he had labored so long and so well.[5]

FUNERAL ORATION DELIVERED BY DR. I. V. BRYANT, PASTOR OF THE FIRST BAPTIST CHURCH, HUNTINGTON, WEST VIRGINIA

Master of Ceremonies, Fellow Citizens and Teachers, I assure you that I am called on today to perform one of the saddest duties of my life. When I remember the intimate acquaintance as well as the relationship existing between Mr. Jones and myself, it is with considerable reluctance as well as emotion that I undertake this task. Yet being invited by the family I respond to their wishes as best I can.

I am reminded in this connection of the words of our Blessed Savior in John, 17th chapter and 4th verse, where he said in that memorial prayer, "I have glorified Thee on the earth. I have finished the work which Thou gavest me to do."

You will bear in mind with me, that the work assigned our Savior was immeasurably greater and more difficult than was in any other instance ever assigned to man. Yet he failed in no respect whatever. From the beginning to the close of his earthly life, he never performed an act, never uttered a word, never had a thought or emotion that varied from the will of God—the perfect standard of Right.

There was nothing in his youth or manhood, nothing in his public or private life, nothing in his most retired actions or innermost movements of his heart that was not perfectly pleasing to God. In his whole frame of mind he was so pure and holy until the most subtle and powerful temptation produced no irregular thought or emotion. Thus through labor and suffering, care and responsibility, He proceeded to Calvary, where on the cross, in anguish of body and spirit, forsaken by His disciples, and worse, by His God, He finished His work.

Be it far from me today, my friends, to liken any man, even the most diligent and faithful to this holy Savior. Yet true Christians are in reality followers of Jesus. They love and obey the same law He loved and obeyed, they love that moral purity which He possessed without mixture. In this way, though imperfect and with faltering steps, they do in their humble way and measure glorify God on the earth and thereby accomplish the great object of their existence.

Through the constant aid of the Holy Spirit they so far finish the work which God gave them to do that they are through Christ accepted of Him and as good and faithful servants admitted into the rewards of His grace.

It was in this qualified sense that the Apostle Paul said when the time of his departure was at hand. "I have fought a good fight. I have finished my course. I have kept the faith." It is also in this sense, my beloved brother whose funeral we are here to attend today, could we doubt not, adopt the language of the text and say, "I have glorified Thee on earth. I have finished the work Thou gavest me to do."

With reference to Prof. J. McHenry Jones, this is either appropriate or inappropriate. But let me say here, that in order to properly glorify God on earth several things are necessary. If he met these pre-requisites, then the words are appropriate. If he did not they are inappropriate.

The first of these requirements is a good, private, Christian character. By this I mean a kind and amiable disposition, and upright, blameless conduct in domestic and social life. This is essential to prepare any man for the important stations of public life.

The life and character of J. McHenry Jones happily met this requirement. He had that combination of intellect and moral qualities which constitutes a useful citizen. His understanding was lucid and discriminating, his imagination fertile and remarkably chaste. While his heart was susceptible of strong and tender emotions, his habit of reasoning was logical and convincing, and his taste uncommonly pure and classical. He felt a disgust for all affected grandeur and floridness of language, to everything which savored of pomp or ostentation. His style was simple, neat, perspicuous and dignified, suited to convey to his hearers the clear and orderly conceptions of his own cultivated mind. He was endowed with an instinctive discernment of what was just and proper, whether in thought or expression. In respect to both words and phrases he employed, and to their arrangement and sense, he always spoke in pure English. From boyhood to mature manhood, Prof. Jones was noted for his strict adherence to business. In every part of the business which he undertook, he evinced a remarkable degree of practical wisdom. In regard to any object which was brought before him, he would inquire not only whether it was good in itself but whether it was practical. It was by no means uncommon for those who associated with him in important public transactions to distrust their own opinions as soon as they found it to be different from his. He exhibited politeness without affectation, dignity without pride, and strict adherence to rules of order without pertinacity. With these qualifications he was often called to preside over public assemblies. The manner in which he presided here and elsewhere was always unexceptional and satisfactory. Who ever had reason to suppose that he thought more highly of himself than he ought to think? When and where did he ever expect an honor which others were not ready to bestow upon him, or manifest a feeling that he was not held high enough among his brethren? He was so evidently unassuming that, although he was always in all societies placed among the first in point of influence, no one envied him or felt that his talents or services were valued too highly.

As to Christian character, it would be difficult for me to name a man of more unquestionable piety. I have known him from childhood to manhood. Even when a small youth he showed unmistakable signs of genuine piety. Even before he was old enough to attend public school he showed indications of a burning thirst for knowledge. At the public school he stood at the head of his class in every branch of study. While even a boy he exhibited characteristics uncommon to childhood. He sought the company of men instead of boys. Professors of schools, ministers of the gospel and men of matured minds were his companions. While yet a boy in tender years he was ordained to preach the gospel and held great audiences spellbound. I have carefully watched his career and have been in close touch with him all during these years. His whole life has been one of an upward march.

He has measured arms with the intellectual giants of this great country. He crossed the ocean and mingled with the highest types of foreign lands, was there weighed in the balance but was not found wanting. As a teacher he has been one unbroken chain of success. He has taught for over thirty years to my personal knowledge and to my recollection has spent that time in three different schools. In this he glorified God on earth and finished his work. He was an uncompromising champion of the rights and privileges of his race. Like Moses he refused to wear an Egyptian crown while Israel groaned beneath the golden chains. His voice has been heard from the Atlantic to the Pacific, from the lakes to the gulf. In newspapers and magazines his pen has figured on every great occasion in this country. He begged no one for a hearing, but like Lovejoy said, "I will be heard." You will all agree with me that from his first introduction to you as president he has had a deep and habitual impression of his great responsibility as an officer of this institution. For his pupils he cherished a sincere and paternal affection. He was always solicitous for their improvement, morally, socially, and intellectually.

He has so lived and walked and ruled in your midst until you are compelled to look back from man and womanhood as you shall occupy the exalted stations of life and say truly there were giants in those days. The Lord grant that the surviving professors, and all their successors in office, and all whose duty it may be to guard and advance the welfare of this institution, may keep in mind the paramount importance of preparing men and women for future usefulness and practical goodliness. We are so constituted that we cannot repress our grief when a good man dies. Society feels the vacuum when an educated mind is withdrawn from its service forever. We feel today that a great hurricane has swept through the forest of humanity and a stately tree has fallen. With us in person, Prof. J. McHenry Jones is no more. He has glorified God on earth. He has finished the work God gave him to do. He has no part nor lot in all that is done under the sun. No more for him the song of love, the voice of gladness, the cup of sorrow and the load of care. No more for him the beauty of spring, the splendor of summer, the glory of autumn, the uncrowned majesty of winter.

Swift flying wheels have borne him from our presence to return no more. The swift flying wings with which his spirit took flight, the chrysalis felt the rays of the sun which called it into being, heard the prancing steeds of God's fiery chariot fresh from the livery of Glory passing through the hall of His dwelling, broke through its bounds and rose up from earthly conditions to those luminous spheres where higher destinies awaited its approach. His body will soon rest in yonder city of the dead overlooking the city of the living where the cedar and weeping willow will sing requiems over him as long as time endures. But "he has glorified God on the earth, he has finished the work God gave him to do."

Brethren, sisters, and friends, permit me to say that a man has been taken from among us of rare excellence of character, a man whose amiable disposition, pious example and diligent, unremitting services have been and will be an inestimable blessing to this institution as well as to the cause of Christ. Our first duty under this afflictive dispensation is cordial, peaceful and entire submission to God, the only all wise, whose dispensations are perfect and right.

In this visitation of his providence God has come to this bereaved widow and these surviving brothers, as well as to this institution and a host of friends. The loss they feel today I shall not attempt to describe. But you will utter no words of complaint, nor give place to any feelings of disquietude. You know that the Lord God omnipotent reigneth, and does His will, and that His will is always just and right. My prayer for you is that God may strengthen you in your affliction. In our tender grief the question will arise. "What shall we do without our true and tried friend?" The answer is "Blessed be God, our rock" and pray for grace which will be sufficient for us. With these few thoughts we bid Prof. J. McHenry Jones farewell.

Time will roll on in its stately march to the judgment; flowers will spring up upon his grave; the storm will spend its fury upon it; morning will greet it with its earliest light; night will crown it with her stars; and the earth rolling in her great orb of infinite space will bear his dust with hers until the mighty archangel of the skies shall blast the last expiring breath of time and the infant cry of an eternity shall begin.

The immortal Garfield once said, "A noble life crowned with heroic death rises above and outlives the pomp and glory of the mightiest empires of earth."

Such a life was that of J. McHenry Jones. Yea, when the history of the world's greatest benefactors shall have been written, the volume will be incomplete without the name of this honored servant of God and his people. He has reared a monument more lasting than brazen statues, more enduring than marble shafts, and higher than the royal pyramids which cannot be destroyed by wasting rains or sweeping hurricanes, the series of countless ages or the flight of eternal years. Let us imitate this noble example. Do you ask me how? I will answer in the language of the immortal Bryant, "So live that when the summons comes to join that innumerable caravan which moves to that mysterious realm where each shall take his chamber in the silent halls of death. Thou go not like the quarry slave at night scourged to his dungeon, but sustained and soothed by an unfaltering trust, approach thy grave like one who wraps the drapery of his couch about him and lies down to pleasant dreams."

A EULOGY BY W. L. HOUSTON, GRAND MASTER OF
THE
GRAND UNITED ORDER OF ODD FELLOWS

My Friends:

I have journeyed from Chicago, that I might for the brethren everywhere pay a simple tribute of reverence to this our beloved dead.

Today in the temple of Odd Fellowship there is great mourning because a mighty one has fallen. Brother J. McHenry Jones was the idol of this order, and the news of his death brought grief and woe to the hearts of all. As he was always the apostle of cheer, and mirth and health, we thought of him as in full strength and never dreamed that for him the tranquil shadows of twilight were falling, and the road had neared its ending so that when the tidings came that he had passed over the purpled hilltops that rear their viewless crests betwixt life and eternity, we felt a shock, the like of which seldom comes to men.

In every avenue of life in which brother Jones put forth effort he became great. He was a great Odd Fellow, and had within the order a career, full, rounded and complete. He rose from the lowest position in his lodge, where the white yoke hung about his neck, until at length he stood at the summit and wore the golden chain of Grand Master, the emblem of authority over four hundred thousand people. And what a Grand Master he was; with his wonderful personality he aroused the enthusiasm and won the admiration of the men and women who wore the emblem of the order upon their breasts. But before he reached this office he achieved the honor of being the first fraternal delegate sent by America to English shores. In 1896 the delegates to the B.B.C., desiring to send greetings abroad, selected brother Jones as the living exponent of Odd Fellowship to bear the message of loyalty and love to our brethren across the sea. And over there with his burning words of eloquence he forged more firmly the links which bind us to those who gave our order birth. He was great as an educator; this West Virginia Colored Institute will be his lasting monument; the record made by the students of this place, as a result of his teaching and influence, will keep bright his fame, undimmed by the gloom of his dismal grave. He was great as a race man and as a citizen of this commonwealth; his undisputed leadership of the race in West Virginia and the esteem accorded him by people in every station gave positive proof of the place he held. He was great as an orator; let no one attempt to describe his power of speech; you knew it and I knew it; oh, how often has he unfolded the pinions of his eloquence and with them widespread has lifted us upward and upward to the rapturous heights where only broad and sweeping wings can soar.

I can attest what Reverend Waters said a moment ago about his tenderheartedness. You know the greatest men are the tenderest. I recall an occasion when brother Jones and I were walking down the streets of Philadelphia he was talking about the sufferings of the Jews in Russia, the persecutions and oppressions they were enduring, and expressed in the most feeling way how his heart went out in sympathy to those downtrodden people in the Czar's domain. Soon we saw a bird on the ground with a broken wing and a dog near it frightened the little thing; brother Jones gently picked it up, carried it to his room and said he could not bear to see the wounded sparrow lying there helpless at the mercy of the dog. I thought then how great was his heart that embraced alike a wronged race in a distant land and a wing-broken bird down in the street. The stream of his sympathy never ran dry, but freely flowed out to all that suffered, whether man or beast or bird.

On the throne of his affections he placed his wife and gave to her the crown of queen; she adored him in turn and let him know the worth and wealth of heart; her devoted care during his sickness, all the day long, and all the night long, is another sweet story of a woman's love.

To her and the members of his family whom he loved and left behind, I tender the sympathy of the Odd Fellows the wide world over and offer them the consolation of the truth, that

There was never a cross so heavy
But the nail scarred hands are there
Out-stretched in tender compassion
The burden to help us bear;
There was never a heart so broken
But the loving Lord can heal,
For the Heart that was pierced on Calvary
Doth still for His loved ones feel.

PRESIDENT J. McHENRY JONES, A.M., LITT. D.,
SCHOLAR AND TEACHER

by Ex-Governor Geo. W. Atkinson

When the news came to me that President James McHenry Jones, the head of the leading colored college, or Institute as it is called, of my native state of West Virginia, had passed to the unseen and into the Great Beyond, I was shocked and grieved, because I had not been advised of his serious illness. It was my pleasure to know him first as principal of Lincoln Public School in Wheeling, where he remained, if my memory is correct, for thirteen years and during all that time his services were entirely satisfactory to the Board of Education of that city. A vacancy occurred in the West Virginia Colored Institute, and the Regents sought about for an established educator to fill the vacancy, and Prof. Jones was unanimously chosen for the place. I write hurriedly, but my recollection is, this took place during my term as governor of the state, but whether it was or not, I know I endorsed him as a suitable and worthy man to become president of that growing institution of learning for the colored race. He was, as I have stated, chosen unanimously by its Board of Regents, and from that time to the day of his death, which covered a dozen or more years, his administration was a pronounced success. Under his management the Institute grew to be one of the best known schools for the higher education of the colored young men and women in the entire south. Therefore as a teacher, executive officer and administrator of an educational institution of the higher grades, he was universally recognized as unusually successful. Taking him, all in all, his equal as an all-around educator could hardly be found. He was a teacher, per se, and among all of the natural orators of West Virginia, and I think I know them all, he had but few equals and I do not believe he had a superior. Indeed, I may safely say, as an orator, white or colored, he was absolutely peerless, and I say this with a personal acquaintance with Dr. Booker T. Washington, the leader of the colored race in America, from his early boyhood to the present writing. In addition to this I can only say truthfully that I never knew a more thorough Christian gentleman than James McHenry Jones; and all of us (white or black) who knew him personally, universally respected him for his merits, his attainments and his worth. Some men are big in body, some in brains, some in usefulness and good nature—Professor Jones was big in all of them. The passing of such a man is just cause for regret and grief, because he will be sadly missed by his associates and friends and by the West Virginia Colored Institute also, for we must all admit that his place will be difficult to fill.

Prof. Jones was a teacher and gave his life, his entire time, to the noblest of callings. In general the teacher's is a low-paid profession, and if many satisfactions did not come to him besides the money he earns, the chairs of many of our colleges and universities would be vacant today. But numerous satisfactions come to him besides the salary he is paid. He takes delight in imparting knowledge to his pupils, and he is rewarded by the public consideration which attends his work. He is also stimulated because he knows that his profession tends, in a greater degree than any other agency, to the wholesale improvement of human conditions. President Eliot once said in an address to teachers at Harvard: "The possibility of making disciples to carry on and better one's work in the world is one of the great satisfactions in life, and this the educator has in great measure. It is a great privilege to anyone to have his acquisitions of thought and learning go down the centuries, multiplied in fruitfulness as they go."

If Prof. Jones were alive today I feel confident he would endorse the following recent utterance of Harvard's great president:

After all, the main inducement to the profession of education as a life work is the delights of the life. To my thinking the career of the educator is the happiest, the most intellectual and the most rewarding as regards service ability and the visibility of the service of all professions. For a young man of foresight I recommend the profession of teaching as the one in which he will realize the chief pleasures of life.

These utterances, in a measure, explain why teachers love their work and why our friend Jones never even thought of abandoning his calling as a teacher.

Prof. Jones was too backward, too retiring to place himself in the rank of great men; and yet, in many ways he was truly great. He was great in heart, great in kindliness, great in sympathy, great in generosity, great in manliness, great in his calling, great in the affections of his pupils, great in his conception of home life; but he abhorred the ordinary term of greatness as accepted by the masses as to what true greatness is. He was altogether another type of man than that. He believed that true greatness is true goodness; that the truly great man is not the one who fills the highest position in the gift of his fellows and commands the greatest acclaim of the people, but rather the one who does the most to make men peaceful and happy, and to make the world sweeter, nobler, grander, better. This was his conception of true and lasting greatness, and in this I think he was forever right.

When Prof. Jones graduated from a high school sometime in the eighties, such institutions were less useful, less powerful, less potential than now. Many branches now taught were infants then. Geology was an infant. Chemistry was a baby compared with the present. Biology was barely at the beginning of its development; and so it may be said of anthropology, archaeology and a dozen other sciences. Then sociology was scarcely dreamed of. But he as a student and a teacher kept in line and was generally at the front of the procession of progress. He, however, was not as aggressive as he was progressive. He was strong in self-reliance but weak in self-assertion. He was too timid to push himself forward and to force others, less equipped, to recognize his real merits and his worth. He was ever kind and was as gentle as a woman. Contentiousness was foreign to his makeup. He conceded to his friends and associates the right to differ from him, but he hewed to the line of duty with a tenacity of purpose rarely found in men. He was not like the inconstant moon, forever changing, but he was like the glorious sun, forever shining.

His religion was a real and practical thing. He found his creed in the Sermon on the Mount rather than in the dusty tomes of theologians, and he possessed the happy faculty of inspiring those whom he taught and loved with his own confidence and enthusiasm. His personality was strong, but gentle; tactful, yet determined; resourceful, but prudent; freely lending his own strength to lighten the burdens of others. Those who knew his voice and the clasp of his hand need nothing to remind them of what he was and what he did, and will hold those traits in lasting and grateful remembrance. In character, morals, manliness and virtue he was as firm and unchanging as a mountain or a rock. More than this, his judgment was of a high order, hence he rarely made mistakes. The writer of these lines knew him from his early manhood well, and upon all important questions rarely found him wrong. He was conscientious to a fault, and therefore could at all times be fully trusted.

Those of us who knew Prof. Jones intimately can truthfully say that he was born for friendships. Affectionate, sincere, optimistic, gracious in manner, mirth-loving, sympathetic, he laid hold on men with a strong grip. In him the teacher never obscured the man, and it is, after all, the man whom we shall best love to recall. He was a man of one work—"This one thing I do," and he rarely failed to do it and do it well. His chief idea was that the work of a college, or high grade academy, like the one over which he presided at the time of his demise, was to make men, real men and not to veneer them. His career was between the old and the new college, and he believed in both; and yet he was slow in giving up very much of the old. He thought as many of us do, that the old-time college more than those of modern years, strove to send out men of power, men of rugged Christian character. He feared that too many of our modern schools aim only to graduate specialists. The dominating purpose, Prof. Jones thought and taught, should in all high grade schools of learning be the symmetrical development of the whole man; the placing of the telescope to the eye of the student so he could see the wide fields of knowledge thus fitting him to use his full powers, developing in him high ideals of character and inspiring him for world service and leadership.

While he loved athletics, yet his idea of a man was not for colleges to turn out quarterbacks and pitchers only, but rather to give training that will produce scholars, thinkers, reformers, world-movers. He believed the college to be a failure unless it graduates first class men as well as first class scholars and high grade athletes. I am sure I represent him correctly in these important matters.

Some men die early, others later on. Pres. Jones laid down his trusts just as the sun reached its noon, while others are permitted to tarry among the living until the shades of evening-tide gather full upon them; but one and all must, without dissenting, lay his armor down when the Master bids him to come or go. Now that Pres. Jones has gone into the beyond, having served his day and generation faithfully and well, we know it is well with him today, and all that is left for us to do, is to sprinkle tears and scatter flowers upon his grave, and to mourn because he is gone.

The supreme lessons of the hour are the lesson of duty, the lesson of uprightness, the lesson of consecration, the lesson of integrity, the lesson of devotion to the unseen. His life was an example to all men. His death was a triumph of faith. His memory is a benediction, especially to the surviving members of his race. He taught and preached the existence of a God, an eternity and heaven. He also taught that life is but a bubble upon the waves of time which we see for a moment and it is gone; that we look and wonder and are lost in the mystery of what is and what is yet to come; that we stand upon a summit and look out into the future and are amazed at the emptiness of vision and as we thus stand, the clouds lower and we see no more. But God rises in the distance and says, "I am the way," and the gloom lifts and we look and live. He was truly a man of faith. He was respected by his neighbors and was esteemed highly by all who knew him well. Charming in his manner and ways, every acquaintance became a friend, and every friend deplores his death.

His funeral was held in the college chapel where he had met the student body and where he had toiled so long and well, and each student threw upon his bier a flower of gratitude and love.

So the watching is ended at home;
Yet a whisper of peace
Bids the flowing tears to cease,
For to wait and to toil—yea, to toil and to wait,
Is earth's passport to Rest within heaven's fair gate.

The sun of J. McHenry Jones has forever set behind the horizon of our view, but the memory of his just, virtuous, upright life will linger as a beautiful twilight in the recollections of all who knew him. Peace to his ashes, rest to his soul.

A TRIBUTE BY HON. H. C. McWHORTER, OF THE WEST VIRGINIA SUPREME COURT OF APPEALS

On our recent visit to the west at Seattle we took in the convention of the International Epworth League of the Methodist Episcopal church, the Methodist Episcopal church, South, and the Methodist Episcopal church of Canada. On the third day of the convention, addresses were made by speakers from all the churches represented, on the topic, "The Epworth League and the Enthronement" [of Christ], Prof. J. McHenry Jones of Charleston being one of the speakers. This was Prof. Jones's last appearance before a public audience; the hall was crowded to its utmost capacity, and although he was the last speaker but one, and the hour was getting late, and the people wearied, he held that vast audience of 6,000 or 8,000 in undivided attention to the close of his magnificent address, which was thought by many to be the best and most eloquent made on that occasion. I heard very many expressions to that effect. We were made to feel proud of West

Virginia. As Prof. Jones has just passed away, I think it due to his memory to say this of the last speech of his life.

H. C. McWHORTER

AN ESTIMATE OF J. McHENRY JONES BY GOVERNOR WM. E. GLASSCOCK

Speaking over the remains of Dr. Jones, Gov. Wm. E. Glasscock, in part, said:

I have known Prof. Jones for fifteen years and my estimate of him is that he was a big-hearted, broad-minded, well-educated, patriotic citizen. He was a good public speaker, but few, if any, I have heard were better, but the best work he did, that which will leave the most lasting impression, was his endeavor to make the world better by his having lived in it. Always his hands, heart, and mind were engaged in lifting up his fellowman, in making smoother the path of adversity, and throwing the light of knowledge into the dark corners of ignorance. His idea of life was to make the world better and happier.

He is gone, and while he has done a good work, this institution over which he presided with such marked credit will continue to increase in usefulness and grow bigger and better with each passing year. It is expected of you who have come into contact with him and have the advantage of that contact to do bigger and better things. His life and work will be speaking to the students of this institution and those who have gone out into the world long after the poignant sorrow caused by his death shall have been erased from their memories. Life is better because of his having lived, and we are fortunate in that we knew him.

RESOLUTIONS ADOPTED BY THE FACULTY OF THE WEST VIRGINIA COLORED INSTITUTE

Whereas, It has been the pleasure of the Almighty, to call from labor to reward our revered president and friend, J. McHenry Jones; and,

86

Whereas, his life has been devoted to the education of his people, working at all times for their best interest, and for the production of useful God-fearing citizens; and

Whereas, In his crossing the bar, the West Virginia Colored Institute has lost a faithful father, the State a useful citizen, and the race a great leader,

Be it resolved, that we the faculty of the West Virginia Colored Institute out of respect and reverence for our late president pass the following resolutions:

1st. That as an educator, President Jones, was a man of culture, of broad and considerate views, and a man whose influence was felt throughout the Nation.

2nd. That as President of the West Virginia Colored Institute, he was steadfast to one ideal—that of making the Institute the greatest possible force for good to the race, and to the State.

3rd. That in his relation to the faculty, he endeavored to act in such manner as to look kindly upon the errors of each, to commend their virtues and to exhibit those rare traits that stamped him as a leader.

4th. That he was a Christian gentleman, and by precept and example strove to extend the Kingdom of the Father and to prove that He is ever ready to save those that trust Him to the uttermost.

5th. That we extend our heartfelt sympathy to his widow in her hour of sorrow and loneliness, knowing that she will miss his companionship, his clinging love and protection, and to his affectionate brothers and weeping relatives.

6th. That these resolutions be published in the *Advocate*, the *Gazette*, the *West Virginia School Journal*, *McDowell Times*, *Pioneer Press*, *The Educator*, and that they be made a part of the permanent records of the School, and that copies be sent to the members of the family.

W. H. LOWRY
CHAS. E. MITCHELL
I. R. WHIPPER, M.D.
FANNIE C. COBB
MARGARET M. LOWRY
BYRD PRILLERMAN
S. H. GUSS
E. M. BURGESS
CHARLOTTE R. CAMPBELL
AUSTIN W. CURTIS

SOLOMON BROWN
JOSEPH W. LOVETTE
JAMES R. PATTON
MAUD JACKSON
JESSIE F. EMBRY
MARY EUBANK
ALBERT G. BROWN
E. A. DORSEY
J. M. CANTY
GEORGE COLLINS

RESOLUTIONS OF THE STATE BOARD OF REGENTS

At a meeting of the State Board of Regents at Morgantown, West Virginia, on the twenty-seventh day of October, 1909, the following order was passed:

IN MEMORY OF J. McHENRY JONES

Ordered that the following preamble and resolutions in memory of J. McHenry Jones, deceased, late President of the Colored Institute at Institute be adopted.

Whereas, in the death of Prof. J. McHenry Jones the State loses the services of one who contributed much during the past thirty years to the upbuilding of its educational system; and,

Whereas, during his administration of eleven years, the West Virginia Colored Institute showed marked improvement in efficiency by the elevation of its standards, the increase in its attendance and the enlargement of its equipment; and,

Whereas, by his upright life and devotion to duty he has left an example worthy of emulation; therefore be it

Resolved, That we recognize in his death the loss to our State of a great factor for good.

Resolved, That in appreciation of and as a permanent memorial of his services we recommend the erection of a tablet, suitably worded, in the walls of the main building of the West Virginia Colored Institute.

Resolved, That we deeply sympathize with his bereaved wife and tender to her and the members of his family our sincerest condolence.

Resolved, That as a further mark of our esteem for his memory we spread these resolutions upon our minutes and that a copy be sent to his widow.

A copy from the records. Attest:

P. W. MORRIS
SECRETARY

THE EPWORTH LEAGUE AND THE ENTHRONEMENT
OF CHRIST

"The Service"
Being Extracts from the Address (his last) Delivered Before the Eighth
International Convention of the Epworth League at Seattle, Washington, July 8,
1909:

The question seems to be, in what way can the Epworth League by its service, contribute to the Enthronement of the Christ? It is not enough that we be called and equipped but that we give ourselves to the work of making the teachings of the Master the supreme force in the direction of the world's affairs.

During his sojourn among men the Master Himself said, "And I, if I be lifted up from the earth will draw all men unto myself."

It, therefore, appears that the chief work of all Christians is to lift high the Christ, bring His life into fuller view, make his work more manifest until the great heart of the universe throbs with adoration at the sound of His name. As the sun gives light and warmth and life to our physical world, so Christ gives light and life to the moral world for He is the light of the world.

The great problems, challenging the profoundest thought; questions of state that have unsettled the foundation stones of national life and embittered the stream of international relationship; social disorders which threaten the existence of the present compact, all find a simple solution when subjected to the light emanating from the glowing words of the lowly Nazarene. It is only through the predominance of the Christ idea that the circle of brotherhood will continue to increase, and justice and equality, the dream of the ages, reach universal application.

Men need a saving sight of the Master, they must be induced to look and live in order that they be transformed into His likeness. We unconsciously become like those we most admire. If by observing the serene expression of the Great Stone face from youth to old age the good man finally resembled it, how much more will looking into the benign countenance of the Christ, living in close proximity, imitating his life and inculcating his character, make men like Him.

In the first place, no service can be fully acceptable that does not begin right. The empire of our King is an invisible one. The Kingdom of Heaven is in you. His rule is void of the ordinary trappings and insignia of earthly powers. His servants, therefore, must enter the army by the sanction of heaven, they must be regenerated or born from above. They must have on their foreheads the kiss of the Holy Ghost, if they would have on their service the blessings of God.

The Enthronement of Christ, fellow Leaguers, depends upon our wisdom to win souls for His cause. Men must humbly, but cheerfully acknowledge His way and lovingly bend under His yoke. Take my yoke and learn of me. See how I do.

A man's world consists of the number of persons and objects in which he is interested. While we all live on the same globe, we do not necessarily live in the same world. The cause which thrills every fiber of my being, may appeal but indifferently to your heart, and, so, the underlying thought which is the mainspring of your ambition may have but little influence on my life. Your struggle and mine, while one in purpose, may be as different as night and day. We must each labor to overcome our own little world, to bring the life and light of an Enthroned Savior to act imperatively in our sphere of influence. "We must work in our own appointed sphere and wish it none other than it is." I must carry the story of a Savior, to the backward, the hated, the discouraged. I must struggle to make them forget their complaints in the thought that earth has no sorrow, that Heaven cannot cure. I must make them see that the powerful hand that made the world is so gentle that the bruised reed it will not break and the smoking flax it will not quench.

Each Epworthian must feel that he is divinely called and sent to forward the Enthronement of the Christ. It helps in the midst of the heat and burden of the day, to feel that I am on the King's business, I have royal authority for my action. He sent them into the vineyard. If we would enthrone the King we must give ourselves unreservedly to his cause. We must not waste effort thinking of ourselves, for selfishness is often the cloud that hides from us the Sun of Righteousness. Knowing our authority and certain of our equipment there is but little reason that we should go limping to the battlefield. We have orders to contend for the coronation of our King, to fight in our part of the field. "For it is ours not to reason why, ours but to do and die." Earnest men care little for sacrifice, not even for death.

The service is, to produce, through Christ, men and women of perfect character. "Character is a unity and all of the virtues must grow in harmony." This harmonious development of the completely fashioned will must be aided by the Spirit of God. All that there is in the Bible, all that there is in the world, is simply an exposition of character of the God who made and created them. To teach men to keep the soul in adjustment with the Eternal, to supply the conditions necessary to produce character, is the heart of the service.

Methods must change with the demands of the age. What would reach men in the sixteenth century may not reach them today. Religion does not change but the manner of appeal to men must vary with the nature of the people and the character of the age. We are appealing to our young people to be something, "to be, rather than to seem". Not simply copies of their neighbors, but conforming to their neighbors' higher ideals so long as those ideals conform to the law and spirit of right.

Neither Saxon Christianity nor Saxon civilization can make of my race a simple reflex in ebony of itself. Race ideals and race distinction must not be ignored. The excellent work of Secretary I. Garland Penn, could not have been accomplished if the church had not granted him the largest liberty in the methods to be pursued. He must use the means best adapted to reach the people. He must use his own weapons in his contention for the King. The service with us is to urge not only the necessity to be something, but also to do something useful. The Master has no use in heaven or earth for a lazy do-less people. A man's religion is often more evident in the way he weeds the garden than in the way he sings a psalm. Religion is a life, and what we do measures our devotion to God. The service is not only to be something and do something but to have something. The old notion that we are especially loved of Heaven because we are poor, has given place to the better notion that God loves us because we are pure. We are not teaching a religion devoid of proper emotion, a soulless materialism, but we are striving to eliminate emotion, the muscular product and to properly care for the blessings God puts into our hands. We do not agree with the demand to stop singing, "You may have all the world, give me Jesus." We are saying as long as there is an unfed human being in the world, to waste is sin. We are coming to see that a farmer is often of as much use to the world as a reformer and that conscientiously plowing a straight furrow forwards the Enthronement of Christ.

The service is the regeneration of the masses. The route is from the college to the crowd. The man with the hoe must be reached and enlightened. The body of death that hangs around the neck of respectability in my race must be called back to life, must be quickened and saved by introducing Caliban to Cadmus. . . .

Jesus Christ saved men by coming in touch with them. He did not sweep like an angel of light away from the crowded streets where men struggled and sinned, away from the hovels where men suffered for bread, away from the seamy side of life and bid us behold Him in all His glory, but down in the midst of the crowd where men sweated blood, in hearing of the groans of the oppressed and dying, He made His way, too busy doing good to think of the grime that might cling to His garments.

We are often so good that we are really worthless, so constantly on guard at our own door that we are of no possible use to the rest of the army.

The cloister has its uses but true warfare is upon the firing line. Our powers must be daily renewed in the closet but the practice is gained in the market place, in the business center, in contact with men.

IN MEMORIAM

NOTES

1. According to Bickley (1989), J. McHenry Jones earned a "first class" teaching certificate after graduating high school. He then attended the University of Michigan and Mt. Hope Episcopal College in Alliance, Ohio. Later, in recognition of his success, he received honorary degrees from Wilberforce University, Rust College, and the West Virginia Baptist Seminary and College.

2. Bickley (1989) reported that Jones was appointed head of the College at Institute by Gov. George Atkinson when the school was eleven years old. It had been established under the Morrill Act as the land grant school for blacks in West Virginia. In 1898 the Institute had fledgling academic and normal departments, plus industrial, agricultural, and trade specialties. Jones quickly made improvements. Bickley notes that during Jones's tenure at Institute, the curriculum was modernized, and the enrollment more than doubled. Four new buildings were erected, twenty acres were added to the real estate holdings, and the school was brought to the attention of the public on a national basis due to Jones's travel and speaking engagements.

3. Bickley provides a discussion of the plot and characters of *Hearts of Gold*. She notes that it is artificial in language and circumstances are stretched to accommodate the ideals of the author. Jones used the novel to discuss topics of the day, such as whether

the South was the best place for blacks to live or whether blacks should remove to Africa. However, Jones made a bold choice in writing about an interracial marriage in 1896. Jones chose to use the term "Afro-American" rather than "colored" more often than not. Moreover, the white grandmother of the heroine built a black identity for her, and black characters were given equal status with white characters.

4. Bickley (1989) adds that along with Samuel Starks and J. C. Gilmer, Jones edited a weekly newspaper published in Charleston called *The Advocate*. Apparently fearing no reprisals, Jones took firm and bold opposition to segregation and other outrages against his race. Furthermore, Jones was active politically. He was selected as alternate-at-large to the 1908 Republican National Convention and helped elect as governor of West Virginia, William Glasscock, whom he saw as an honest man, ready to defend the blacks against the pressures of those who would disenfranchise them.

Discussed neither in the memorial nor by Bickley is the fact that J. McHenry Jones was also a business man. A series of articles in African-American newspapers published during February and March of 1903 tell the story. Jones was a member of the board of directors of the first oil company in the United States to be owned and operated by African-Americans. Jones, along with George A. Myers of Cleveland and Wilbur F. Jones, Ralph W. Tyler, and George A. Weaver of Columbus, bought 73 acres in Morgan County, "the richest oil belt of Ohio." Big companies, owned by whites, had offered large sums for the business, but the men stood fast. In fact, the Wilgera Oil and Gas Company, headquartered in Columbus, Ohio, incorporated under the laws of West Virginia and with a capital stock of $50,000, announced itself publicly only after the deeds were in hand and the company was safely chartered; whites had so often sabotaged such plans by blacks. By March the company had acquired 400-500 more acres in Morgan and Washington Counties, and had at least one gas and one oil well working. Ultimately successful or not (the company's further fortunes were not followed), the very existence of the Wilgera Oil and Gas Company shocked whites and excited blacks with hope.

5. Ancella Bickley (1989) in her monograph on J. McHenry Jones noted that front page coverage was given Jones's death in *The Charleston Gazette, The Wheeling Intelligencer, The*

Wheeling News, The Charleston Advocate, The Colored American, and the *Seattle Republican.* He lay in state in the Hazelwood Assembly Hall of the West Virginia Colored Institute the morning and early afternoon of September 25, 1909. The funeral that afternoon was "one of the largest gatherings of prominent people ever to assemble for the last rites for a black man in West Virginia." The noon train added three special coaches to accommodate the crowd. Among those attending were William Glasscock, Governor of West Virginia; W. L. Houston, Grand Master of the Grand United Order of Odd Fellows; Thomas Hodges and John Shepherd of the State Board of Control; George Laidley of the State Board of Regents; M. P. Shawkey, State Superintendent of Schools; H. C. McWhorter, former Supreme Court judge; J. S. Darst, auditor; and Odd Fellows Lodge members from Charleston and Gallipolis, Ohio. Appended here are the tributes made that day by Gov. Glasscock, Judge McWhorter, Ex-governor George W. Atkinson, and W. L. Houston.

94

REFERENCES

Bryant, I. V. (16 Jan 1922). Letter to C. G. Woodson.

Censuses:
1840 Federal: Raccoon Twp., Gallia County, OH. P. 17 - Reuben Jones.
1850 Federal: Fayette Twp., Lawrence County, OH. P. 88 - Reuben Jones.
1850 Federal: Fayette Twp., Lawrence County, OH. P. 881 - Joseph Jones and William Reed.

REFERENCES, cont'd

Censuses, cont'd:
1860 Federal: Gallipolis Twp., Gallia County, OH. P. 502 - Joseph Jones.
1880 Federal: Jackson Twp., Jackson County, OH. P. 65C - John Jones.
1900 Federal: Monroe Twp., Perry County, OH. P. 142A - John L. Jones.
1900 Federal: Monroe Twp., Perry County, OH. P. 141B - Mary Davis.

Colored Citizen. (19 May 1866). Vol. 3, No. 29 of the Cincinnati newspaper.

Cullinam, P. M. (Ed.). (1909). *The Book of Perry County: An Historic Industrial Portfolio.* New Lexington, OH: The New Lexington *Herald.*

Dempsey, Eileen. (1994). Old church offers faith to folks of dying, tiny village. Columbus *Dispatch* Sunday Magazine, 27 Feb. P. 10.

Felldin, Jeanne R. (1981). *Index to the 1820 Census of Virginia.* Baltimore: Genealogical Publishing Co., Inc.

Fink, Leon. (1983). *Workingmen's Democracy: The Knights of Labor and American Politics.* Urbana: University of Illinois Press.

Fleischman, John. (1993). The Emancipation of Gallia. *Ohio Magazine.* Vol. 16, No. 6. Pp. 74-78.

Frazier, E. Franklin. (1932). *The Free Negro Family: A Study of Family Origins Before the Civil War.* Nashville: Fisk University Press.

Furguson, T. J. (1866). *Negro Education: The Hope of the Race.* Marietta, OH: Tribune Printing.

Gallipolis Journal. (27 Nov 1862). P. 2 (two articles).

REFERENCES, cont'd

Gutman, Herbert G. (1976). Black coal miners and the American labor movement. In Gutman, H. G., *Work, Culture, and Society in Industrializing America: Essays in American Working-class and Social History,* (pp. 119-208). New York: Knopf.

Horton, James Oliver. (1993). *Free People of Color: Inside the African-American Community.* Washington & London: Smithsonian Institution Press.

In Memoriam. Collection of Beulah A. Johnson.

Indianapolis Freeman. (21 Feb 1903). P. 1, Cols. 1 and 2.

_____. (28 Feb 1903). P. 4, Cols. 4 and 5.

_____. (14 Mar 1903). P. 8, Cols. 2 and 3.

Informer. (Urbana, OH). (Feb 1903). P. 3.

Jackson, Luther P. (1942). *Free Negro Labor and Property Holders in Virginia 1830-1860.* New York: Appleton-Century.

Jones, John L., death certificate. (13 May 1938). California Dept of Public Health: Vital Statistics, local register No. 25.

Lammermeier, Paul J. (1973). The urban black family of the nineteenth century: A study of black family structure in the Ohio Valley, 1850-1880. *Journal of Marriage and the Family,* 45. Pp. 440-456.

Lawrence County, Ohio Marriage Book 4. P. 50.

REFERENCES, cont'd

(Laws of Ohio). *The State of Ohio: General and Local Acts & Joint Resolutions Adopted by the 67th General Assembly.* Vol. LXXXIV. (1887). Columbus: State Printers.

Nelson, Charles H. (1986). The town least likely. *Ohio Magazine*, July. Pp. 40-81.

Ploski, H.A. & Williams, J. (1992). *Reference Library of Black America.* Vol. V.

Schreiner-Yantis, Netti & Love, Florence S. (compilers) (1987). *The 1787 Census of Virginia.* Springfield, VA: Genealogical Books in Print.

Sheeler, J. Reuben. (1946). The struggle of the Negro in Ohio for freedom. *Journal of Negro History*, 31. Pp. 208-226.

Shilling, David Carl. (1913). Relation of southern Ohio to the South during the decade preceding the Civil War. *Quarterly Publication of the Historical and Philosophical Society of Ohio*, VIII, No. 1. Pp. 3-19 and appendix A.

Tribe, Ivan M. (1969). Rise and decline of private academies in Albany, OH. *Ohio History*, 78, No. 3. Pp. 188-228.

U.S. report of the Commissioner of Education. (1877-1886/7). *Statistics of Institutions for the Instruction of the Colored Race—Institutions for Secondary Instruction.* Washington, DC: Government Printing Office.

Woodson, Carter G. (1925). *Free Negro Heads of Families in the United States in 1830.* Washington, DC: The Association for the Study of Negro Life & History, Inc.

Wright, Martha. (1976). A very special school. Columbus *Dispatch* Magazine (14 Mar 1976). Pp. 24-26.

INDEX

Abbott, Lyman, 44
Advocate, The (See: *The Charleston Advocate*), 86, 92, 93
Africa, xiii, 36, 47, 57, 68, 91
African Methodist Episcopal Church, 36, 37, 62, 69, 84
Ailshire's Mill, 9
Ailstock, xiii, 2
    Elizabeth, vii, 54, 68
    John, 52
    Joseph, vii, 54, 68
Albany (OH), 13, 14, 59, 60, 68
Albany Manual Labor Academy, 60
Alliance (OH), 91
Alton (IL), xii, 40
Andrews, Thomas, 27
Ardmore (OK), xi, 45
Arnett Bill, The 23, 62
Arnett, Bishop Benjamin William, 62
Athens (OH), 40, 42, 43, 61
Athens County (OH), 60
Athens Messenger, 60, 92
Atkinson, Gov. George, 31, 38, 80, 91, 93
Atwood Institute, 60
Aunt Nelly, 15, 16

B&O Railroad, 42
Bacon, A. M., v
Baptist National Convention, 37
Beatty, Elsie, xiii
    Luke, xiii
Bedford County (VA), xiii
Beechwood Cemetery, Pomeroy (OH), viii, 34
Bell, Ira, 48
Berry, Edwin, 61
Big Bend (OH), 21, 23
Biggs, Ben, 34
Birkimer, John A., 49
Black, James, 25
Black Laws, 61
Blockson, Charles L., v
Bluevaynes, The, 36, 72
Boley (OK), x, xi, 45, 46, 51

Bolton (England), 31, 70
Boone, Jennie, 42, 43
Boston (MA), 48, 54, 68, 70
Bowles, Prof. John Jr., 60
    Rev. John P., 60
Boxwell examination, x, 49
Broadis
    Sadie D. (See: Sarah D.)
    Sara/Sarah D., x, 28-30, 56
    Zenobia (See Zenobia Broadis Jones)
Broadway, 46
Brooklyn Bridge, 47
Brown
    Albert G., 86
    John, xii, xiii
    Scott, 39, 40
    Solomon, 86
Bryan, William Jennings, 49, 77
Bryant
    Abraham, 11
    Charles, 11
    Charlie Jr., 11
    Clara, xiii
    Flem, 11
    Flemmon, xiii
    George, xiii, 6
    I. V., Dr., xiii, 38, 44, 66, 73
    Issac, 66
    James, xiii, 11
    John, xiii
    Joseph, 11
    Mary, xiii, 11
    Sarah, xiii
    William, xiii
Burgess, E. M., 38, 86
Burlington (OH), viii, 6, 7, 56, 66
Butternuts, 13, 17

Cambridge (OH), 27
Camp Meade (MD), 52
Campbell, Charlotte, 38, 86
    James E., 21
Canada, 12, 13, 36, 62, 84
Canty, J. M., 38, 86
Carr, Thomas, 23
Carter, Louis, 24

Case School of Applied Sciences,
    Cleveland (OH), 29
Castle Garden (NY), 47
Cattletsburg (KY), 66
Charleston (WV), 37, 52, 66, 84,
    92, 93
Charleston Advocate, The, 86,
    92, 93
Charleston Gazette, The, 86, 92
Cheap John's, 19
Chicago (IL), xii, 33, 40, 42, 78
Chicago Music College, 45
Chicago, University of, x, 50
Childs, Frank, 50
Chillicothe (OH), 31, 32
Cincinnati (OH), viii, 3-5, 7, 10,
    18, 19, 21, 23, 26, 31, 37, 42,
    43, 60-62, 71
Cincinnati Commercial, 47
Civil War, v, vi, vii, 11, 13, 17,
    52, 59, 62, 93
Clark, W. G., 64
Clark, William E., 64, 65, 66
Claxton, Ed, 27
Cleopatra's Needle (NY), 47
Cleveland (OH), viii, xi, 29, 33-36,
    42, 45, 47-50, 64, 92
Cleveland Gazette, 64
Cobb, Fannie C., 86
Collins, George, 86
Colored American, The, 93
Colored Citizen, 60, 61
Columbia University, 50
Columbus (OH), vii, ix, xiii, 11,
    27-29, 35, 37, 43, 48, 50, 52,
    56, 69, 70, 92
Cincinnati Commercial, 47
Conley, Wm. G., Gov., 41
Connelly
    Richard, 40, 43
    Mrs. Richard, 43
Corning (OH), 63
Corning High School, 50-52
Corning War, 63
Cousions, Henry, 24
    Morris, 24
Creek and Seminole University,
    xi, 45

Curtis
    A. W., 38
    Austin W., 86

Darst, J. S., 93
Davidson, Andrew Jackson, 61
    Olivia, 61
Davis
    Mary, 65, 93
    Prof., 41
    Richard L., 62-65, 92
    Sara Johnson, 58
Dayton (OH), 59
Deavertown (OH), 13
Denison University, 50
Donahue, Judge Morris, 36
Donaldson, Rev., 25
Dorsey, E. A., 86
Douglass National Bank, Chicago
    (IL) 45
Dunbar, P. L., 5
Durst, Sherman, 38

Egypt, 47
El Centro (CA), 50, 56
Eliot, President, 81
Emancipation Day, 13, 58
Emancipation Proclamation, 58
Embry, Jessie F., 86
England, 28, 31, 36, 37, 70, 72
Enterprise Academy, 59-61
Enterprize Landing, Pomeroy
    (OH), 21
Epworth League, 36, 37, 72, 84, 88
Eubanks, Mary E., 28
Eureka Lodge, 69
Evergreen Cemetery, 56

Farmers & Merchants Bank,
    Boley (OK), 45
Ferguson/Furguson, G. E., 41, 60,
    61
    Thomas J. (T. J.), 22, 68
Field, William, 54
First National Bank, Pomeroy
    (OH), 34
First National Bank of Boley
    (OK), xi, 45
Flannigan, Superintendent, 23

Fort Smith (AR), 45
Foster, Governor, 63
France, 52, 72
Frazier, E. Franklin, v
Free Negro, Free Negroes, 1, 3
Free Will Baptist Church,
    Pomeroy (OH), 22, 59, 68
Friendly Society Movement, 70
Fugitive Slave Law, 12, 62

Gallia County (OH), ix, xi, 29, 53,
    55, 58
Gallia County Emancipation Day,
    58
Gallipolis (OH), vi, viii, 3, 6-10,
    12-17, 20, 21, 42, 54, 66, 68,
    93
Gallipolis Journal, The, 16, 57
Gazette, 86
Gee (family), 7
German Salt Company, 34
Gilman, Lieutenant, 57
Gilmer, J. C., 92
Glasscock, William, 38, 85, 92, 93
Goings, Addie, 60
Gouldtown (NJ), v
Gray, Tommy, 13
Greene County (OH), 62
Grosvenor, Charles, 49
Guss
    S. H., 86
    Sherman, 40
Gutman, Herbert G., 49, 62-64, 66
Guyandotte (WV), 66

Hammond, The Rev., 29
Hampton (VA), v
Handy, Bishop, 47
Harner (See: Wm. Ballard
    Harper), 25
Harper
    W. W., 50
    William Ballard, 25
Harper's Ferry (VA), 12
Harris
    Boliver, 25
    Wm., 47

Harrison
    Carrie/Carrier, 27, 31, 69
    William Henry, 8, 72
Hartford City (WV), 21
Harvard University, 81
Haynes
    Edith, xiii
    George/Georgia E., x, 51
Hazlewood
    Albert, 21
    Harry, 22
    J. M., 25, 39
    James Monroe, 38
Hearing, Charles, 49
Hearts of Gold, 36, 71, 72
Henderson, Fletcher, Orchestra,
    xi, 46
Henrico County (VA), 56
Hill
    Edward, vii, 11, 13, 21, 26, 33
    Elizabeth, vii, 11, 13, 21, 26, 33
    Elizabeth Jones, vii, 11, 13,
        21, 26,, 33
    George, vii, 11, 13, 21, 26, 33
    Maria, vii, 11, 13. 21. 26, 33
    Marshall, vii, 11, 13, 21, 26, 22
    Sylvanis, vii, 11, 13, 21, 26, 33
Hocking Valley, 63, 65
Hocking Valley Coal Region, 63
Hodges, Thomas, 93
Holland
    Milton M., 61
    William H., 61
Holmes (family), 7
    Tom, 14, 15
Houston (See: Hueston), W. L.,
    78, 93
Howard University, 66
Hueston (See: Houston), W. L.,
    38
Huntington (WV), 22, 38, 44, 66
Huntington, 22, 38, 44, 66
Hurt, Elijah, 40

In Memoriam, viii, 54, 59, 61
Indian blood, 2, 54, 68
Indianapolis (IN), 70
Indianapolis Freeman, The, v

Institute (WV), v, viii, x, xi, xii,
    31-33, 35-40, 43-44, 49, 50,
    73
Ironton (OH), 17, 66, 69

Jackson County (OH), vii, 11
Jackson, Maud, 86
Jamestown (VA), 1
Jefferson, John R., 22
Jim Crow., 20
Johnson
    Belfield, 6
    Beulah A., 57
    James, 28
    Judge Jas., 49
    Theo., 47
Jones
    Alex, 16, 19, 22, 24-26, 33, 37,
        62, 73
    Alexander, viii, x, 8
    Beulah, 57, 94
    C. E., 22, 38, 39, 42
    Carrie, 27
    Charles, viii, xii, 19, 32
    Charles Connelly, xii, 40, 41
    Charles E./Edward, 44, 73
    Charley, 24, 29, 30, 32, 34, 44-
        46, 50, 73
    Charlie, 32, 39, 42-44, 46, 47
    Claude B., xi, 46
    Earl/Earl R., xi, 44, 47, 52
    Edward, vii, 11
    Edward Francis, xii, 41
    Emma, vii, xiii, 11
    Ethel/Ethel Mae, x, 37, 44, 46,
        50, 51,
    Eula/Eula Fay, xii, 41
    Eunice, xii, 15, 38, 40, 44
    Flem, 11, 24, 26, 29-32, 35, 36,
        44-46, 62, 73
    Fleming, viii, xii
    Fleming B./Fleming Bertram,
        viii, xi, xii, xiii, 21, 44, 45
    Hazel, x, 46
    J. L., 64
    J. McHenry, i, iii, iv, 27, 37, 67-
        69, 72, 74, 76-78, 80, 84-85,
        87, 91, 92
    James Henry, 12

James McHenry, xi, xii, 21, 40,
    44, 54, 55, 59, 61, 65, 66, 68,
    69, 80, 92
James [Mc]Henry (See: James
    McHenry)
John/John L., i, v, vi, vii, ix, xi,
    xiii, xiv, 1, 2, 3, 4, 6, 10, 11,
    19, 21, 51, 52, 53, 54, 55, 56,
    62, 63, 66, 73, 93
John L. Jr., 43, 47
John Lysandrous, viii, x, 10
(John) Marshall, vii
Joseph, vi, vii, viii, xiii, 2-13,
    15, 17, 18, 22, 34, 53, 54, 55,
    56, 57, 66, 68, 92, 93
Joseph Jr., vii
Josephus, viii, 9, 16, 19, 22-24
Lawrence, xiii
Lotus, 45
Lotus, Jr., 45
Louis Earl, xii, 41, 45
Margaret, ix, x, xii, 41, 54, 56
Maria, vii, 11
Marshall, vii, 11
Martha, vii, ix, x, xiii, 2, 4, 54
Mary, vii, viii, ix, xiii, 2, 4, 6,
    40, 43, 44, 54, 55
Mary F. (See: Mary F. Vance)
Mary Francis, xiii
Maurice Reid, xii, xv, 41
McHenry (See: James McHenry
    or J. McHenry)
Mrs. Mayme, xi, 32, 44-46
Octavia, x, 11, 50
Oteria, vii, 11
Reuben, vi, vii, ix, 1-2, 11, 53,
    54, 56, 68, 92
Ruben
Sarah D. (See: Sarah D.
    Broadis)
Sylvanis, vii, 11
Temperance (See: Temperance
    Reid/Reed)
Thomas Jefferson, viii, 22
Tommy, 24
Viola, xi, 52
Wert, x, 33
Wilbur F., 92
William, vii, 8, 9, 11, 53

Jones, *cont'd*
  William Henry/William H.,
    viii, ix, 55
  Zenobia Broadis, x, 30, 35, 43,
    44, 49, 50, 56
Julah's Bromine Works, 25

Kanawha River, 3
Kanawha Valley, 15
Kansas, University of, 51
Kansas City, 51
Kappa Alpha Psi, 41
Karr's Run, Meigs County (OH)
    (See: Kerr's Run), 20
Kelly, Frank A., 49
Kenton (OH), 28
Kentucky, 55, 62, 68
Kerr's Run, Meigs County (OH)
    (See: Karr's Run), 20
Knights of Labor, 26, 63-64
Knights of Pythias, 70
Knights of the Golden Circle, 13

Langston University (Oklahoma
    State), xi, 45
Lawrence County (OH), viii, ix,
    xii, xiii, 12, 17, 53-56, 66, 68,
    92
Lawrenceville (VA), 51
Leaper, Capt., 58
Lee
  Bishop, 57
  J. J., 27
Lewis Academy, 60
Lewis
  Ichabod, 60
  Lamira, 60
  William, 60
Lightburn Retreat, 15
Lincoln, Abraham, 9, 12, 31, 58,
    72
Lincoln Public School, 80
Love
  Fannie Lee, ix, x, 11
  Josephine, ix
  Mary, ix
  Nancy, ix, 56
  Robert, ix, x, 11, 56
  Sally, ix

Love, *cont'd*
  Susanna, ix
  William, ix
Lovette, Joseph W., 86
Lowry
  Margaret M., 86
  W. H., 86
Luther Olsla High School, 45

Macadonia/Macedonia (OH), 12
Marietta (OH), viii, 27, 31, 69
Martin, F. C., 50
Martlesville (OK), 45
Mason (family), 7
Mason Lodge, 70
Massachusetts, 9
McConnellsville (OH), 28
McDonald, Shelly, 49
McDowell Times, 86
McKinley, Gov. William, 48, 49,
    55
McQuig, John, 34
McWhorter
  H. C., Judge, 36,
    84-85, 93
  H. P., 37
Means, A. J., 47
Meharry Medical College, xi, xii,
    40, 45
Meigs County (OH), 30, 55
Memphis (TN), 19
Methodist Episcopal Church, 36,
    69, 84
Metz (France), 52
Meuse Sector (France), 52
Michigan, University of, xi, 29,
    46, 71
Middleport (OH), xi, 22, 26, 30-32
Miners' Cooperative, 29, 64
Miners, coal, 26, 33, 48, 63-66
Mitchell
  Chas. E., 86
  Mrs. Charles, 38
Moats, Irene Chilton, 22
Mobile (AL), 34, 35
Monkey Run (OH), 20
Moore
  Elizabeth, viii, 31, 71
  Mrs., 13, 92

Morgan County (OH), 13, 92
Morgantown (WV), 87
Morrill Act, 71
Morris, Mayme, xi, 32, 36
    P. W., 87
Morton, 72
    Bertha, 22
    Calvin, 21
    Calvin, Sr., 25
    Edward, 22
Moss, Summers, 16
Mt. Hope Episcopal College, 91
Moynihan, Daniel, 59
Myers, George A., 92

N & I School, Institute (WV), 10,
    49
Nailor's Run (OH), 20
Nashville (TN), xi, xii, 40, 45
National Labor Tribune, 64
Nelson, Charles, 64
Nelsonville (OH), 43, 48
New Haven (CN), x, 51, 70
New Lexington (OH), 49, 50
New Orleans (LA), 4
New Richmond (OH), viii, 6, 18-
    21, 42, 68
New River, 63
New York (NY), 46, 47, 50
Norman
    Rachel, vii
    Sarah, vii
Northern Pacific Coal Company,
    65, 66

Oberlin College, 29, 51, 60
Odd Fellows, 27, 28, 31, 37, 38, 69,
    70, 72, 78, 79, 93
Odd Fellows Journal, 72
Ohio, vi, 3, 6, 7, 10-13, 21, 23, 26,
    27, 31, 36-38, 44, 47, 48, 53,
    54, 63, 65, 68, 69, 72, 73, 93
Ohio River, vi, 6, 12-14, 16, 20, 56
Ohio State Medical School, 64
Ohio State University, 27, 51
Ohio University, xii, 40
Oklahoma, 44, 45, 51
Oklahoma Normal & Industrial
    Institute, 45

Oklahoma State, xi, 45
Oklahoma, University of, 45
Olathe (KS), 51
Other Room, The, 44

Pace, Mr., 23
Pacific Land Company, 50
Page, Viola, xi, 52
Parkersburg (WV), 22, 33
Parks
    Bishop, 45
    President, 32
Pasadena (CA), 37, 50
Pasco, Samuel, 49
Patton, James R., 86
Payne
    Octavia, x
    W. A., x, 37, 50
    Zenobia (See: Zenobia Broadis
    Jones)
Penn, I. Garland, 90
Pennsylvania, 31, 72
Perdreau, Michel S., v, vi
Perry County (OH), 26, 29, 55, 65
Phi Beta Sigma, 45
Philadelphia (PA), 47, 79
Pioneer Press, 86
Pittsburgh (PA), 21, 38
Point Pleasant (WV), 3, 6
Pomeroy (OH), viii, x, 6, 9-11, 19-
    22, 26, 28, 33, 34, 36, 42, 68
Pomeroy High School, 23, 27, 68
Portsmouth (OH), 6
Preston, Thomas, 29
Prillerman, Byrd, 38, 86

Red River, 19
Reds (baseball team), 43
Reed (See: Reid)
    George, 6, 55
    James, 6
    James H., 6, 55
    John, 6, 55
    Mary, 5, 55
    Nancy, viii, 6
    Rosetta, 6, 55
    Samuel, 6, 55
    Temperance, viii, 6, 54-55, 7, 8,
    22, 66, 68

Reed, *cont'd*
  William, viii, 6, 7,
  William H., 55
Reid, Temperance (See: Reed)
Rend, Colonel, 63
Rendville (OH), x, xi, xii, 13, 28-
  30, 32, 33, 35, 40, 44, 48, 52,
  55, 62, 63, 64, 65, 66
Republican National Convention,
  92
Rhine River (France), 36
Richmond (VA), 3, 8, 10, 53
Ripley (OH), 6
Roanoke (VA), 63
Rock Spring School, 26
Rockingham County (VA), xiii
Roseland Ball Room, 46
Ross County (OH), 11
Round, Mr., 48
Russia, 79
Rust College, 91
Rust University, 72

St. James (river packet), 20
St. Paul (school), 50
San Antonio (TX), ix, 35
Saulter, Bishop, 47
Scarborough, W. S., 60
Scott, Roxa, 56
Scotland, 72
Seattle (WA), 36, 37, 72, 84, 88
Seattle Republican, 93
Shaw University, 72
Shawkey, M. P., 93
Shawnee (OH), 63
Shelton, Reverend, 5
Shepherd, John, 93
Simpson, Jennie Boone (See:
  Jennie Boone), 42, 43
Simpson Methodist Episcopal
  Church, 69
Slater, Eva L. Jones, xiii
Smith
  Ambrose, 6
  Capt., 57
Smith Opera House, New
  Lexington (OH), 49
Solidy (OH), 7

Southern California, University
  of, x, 50
Southpoint (OH), viii, xi, 6, 7, 17,
  19, 21, 50
Spanish-American War, 52
Spears
  Joe, 21
  Joel, 25
  Uncle Chas., 24
Spriggs, Mr., 38
Springfield (OH), 28
Starks, Samuel, 92
State Bureau of Negro Welfare &
  Statistics, 41
Stevens, Saml, Grocery Co.,
  Columbus (OH), 50
Steward, Theophilus G., v
  William, v
Straitsville (OH), 63
Strange Transformation, A,
  36, 71
Sugar Run, Meigs County (OH),
  20
Summer, Charles, 9
Sunday Creek Coal Fields, 66

Tanner
  Alfred, xiii
  Eliza, xiii
  Emmanuel, xiii
  Mary E., xiii
Texas, 51, 61
Tharp, Geo. P., 49
Thomas, Alma, xi, 46
Thompson (family), 7
351st Field Artillery, Battery F,
  xi, 52
Tolliver
  H. G./Harry, x, 51
  Octavia
Topeka (KS), 51
Tuppins, I. S./Isaiah, 29, 64
Tuskegee Institute, 61
Tyler
  Floyd, 29
  Ralph W., 92

UMWofA, 26, 63, 64 (See: United
  Mine Workers)

UMW Journal, 62, 63, 64
Uncle Toms, 72
Underground Railroad/Railway,
      vi, 12, 13, 56, 57

United Mine Workers of America,
      62, 63, 64
United Order of Odd Fellows, 31,
      38, 69, 70, 78

Valley Forge (PA), 52
Vance, Mary F., xii, 32, 44
Viney (family), 7
Virginia, vi, viii, 1, 4, 7, 17, 29, 55,
      56, 62, 72

Wales, 31, 72
Walker, John, 47
Walker Memorial Baptist Church,
      66
Ward (family), 7
      Joe, 9
Washington
      Booker T., 61, 64, 65, 96, 97
      George, 54, 68, 97
Washington County (OH), 92
Washington Court House (OH),
      47
Washington, DC, 52, 66
Washington (state), 65, 66, 72, 88
Waters, The Reverend, 79
Watson, Lyla C., xi, 45
Wayne, Dave, 43
Weaver, George A., 92
Wesleyan Methodist Church, 22,
      25
West Virginia, xii, 22, 24, 32, 36,
      37, 52, 63, 64, 69, 73, 78, 80,
      84, 85, 92, 93
West Virginia Baptist Seminary,
      91
West Virginia Collegiate
      Institute, 21, 22, 36
West Virginia Colored Institute,
      38, 71, 78, 80, 81, 86, 87, 93
West Virginia School Journal,
      86
West Virginia State College, v,
      viii, x, xi, xii, 21

Western Reserve, 33
Wheeling (WV), xi, 21, 27, 28, 31,
      32, 35, 36, 44, 46, 69, 80
Wheeling Intelligencer, The,
      92
Wheeling News, The, 93
Whipper, I. R., M.D., 86
Whit-week, 31, 70
Wilberforce University, x, xi, 46,
      51, 52, 72, 91
Wilgera Oil and Gas Company, 92
Wilkins, Fannie, 43
Wolverines (baseball team), 43
Woodson, Carter G., 53
World War I, xi, xii, 51, 52
World's Fair, 47
Wright
      Bill, 14
      Edith, 47
      Mr., 33, 35
      Mrs. W. D., 47
      W. B., 33, 50
Wyoming, 33

Xenia (OH), 64

Yale University, x, 51
Yorktown, 54, 68

Zanesville (OH), 52, 69

www.ingramcontent.com/pod-product-compliance
Lightning Source LLC
Chambersburg PA
CBHW071228290326
41931CB00037B/2449